Silence in Schools

Silence in Schools

Helen E Lees

IOEPress

A Trentham Book

Institute of Education Press

Institute of Education Press
20 Bedford Way
London
WC1H 0AL

First published 2012

British Library Cataloguing-in-Publication Data
A catalogue record for this book is available from the
British Library

ISBN 978-1-85856-475-3

Printed by CPI Group (UK) Ltd, Croydon, CR0 4YY

Contents

There is only silence and what is.
The rest is code.

Acknowledgements

Tremendous appreciation goes to the research participants who shared with me their time and expertise of silence in schools in the most generous, professional and welcoming of spirits. Also, a debt of gratitude is owed to the various people met over the course of the past few years who shared their experiences of silence in schooling and more widely, sometimes giving me links to relevant work and useful suggestions.

I would like to thank Gillian Klein at Trentham Books. Her faith in me and support has been special. It is a privilege to work with such a thoughtful, intelligent publisher. I'm grateful to the Laboratory for Educational Theory at the University of Stirling for giving me some time away from daily business to focus on the writing of this book in its early stages and to conduct the interviews.

Thanks to Clive Harber, Nick Peim, David E. Cooper, Deborah Orr, Julian Stern, Duncan Mercieca, Harriet Pattison, David Hartley, Walter Humes, Moira Von Wright, Gert Biesta, Morwenna Griffiths, Paul Standish, Sarah Robinson, Susan Mitchell, Liz Edmunds, Joy Hunter, Ann Lees, Alex Lees and Jim Green for being supportive and encouraging in various ways. Guglielmo, as ever, is a rock and a smile without which I am lessened. Insufficiencies of this text are my own doing and responsibility entirely.

This book, despite and because of its secularity, is dedicated to Swami Vivekananda, who knew what silence was, yet spoke about it for all our sakes.

Preface

Silence is the new oil. From a global perspective, both are sourced and mined with effort from the depths. Both involve a power of transformation that can change the world. Both are complicated in their manifestation. Both are valuable.

> [Oil] has no voice, body, army, or dogma of its own. It is invisible most of the time, but, like gravity, it influences everything we do. (Maass, 2009:7)

Yet there are profound differences. Silence of a positive kind strong enough to bring benefits to people is, unlike oil, a limitless resource. And it is cost free. It is not destructive. To secure it does not come at the price of war and despair, killing, political machination and lies (see eg. Shaxson, 2008). Securing silence as a resource helps bring about the opposite of all this. Silence brings peace, healing, joy, simplicity and truth. It brings about the laying of foundations of understanding.

Our global history with oil has not been easy. It has brought pollution, poverty, and corrupting power and despite its utility, is not that useful for a planet housing people who wish to live in equality, harmony and on a planet that is healthy. What we need is a new 'oil' or, rather, an antidote to the forces things like oil bring into the world. We need a world resource that is the property of everyone, that everyone can use and everyone can live with happily. This resource is silence. Silence strong enough to help and heal.

Nowhere do we need the help of such silence more than in the lives of children in school settings. Whatever is wrong about schooling, silence seems to help set straight and put right. As an intervention of a radical kind, strong silence has the power to transform education in many ways. Future generations will come to rely on it. Unlike oil, silence will not run out or threaten to do so. Its price will not inflate. It will not make us dependent. Instead, it will set us free.

Writing this book has taken me aback. I have been jolted and shocked. Before embarking on this project, I had little awareness of the astonishing qualities silence offers for school education. I was interested and I thought it was important to bring silence into schools. But nothing prepared me for what I discovered as I read about silence in school practice. There's nothing wrong with it as a resource, if it is strong. It is an astonishing educational resource. Silence is not a nothing or a small something for education. It is a punch of immense force.

And so, despite previous deeply and thoughtfully held views that schools are irredeemable, undemocratic, harmful institutions, I now admit and happily concede that schools with strong silence might just be good places. In fact, silence in schools can make schools excellent places to want to be and to experience becoming an educated person.

As a counter-force to over-testing, to prescriptive 'how-to-do-ness', to unending inane and thoughtless 'learning' discourse, to relentless instruction, to tick-boxes, silence cuts through. It restores sanity to schooling. Strong silence in schools creates:

- more democratic environments suited to educative purposes
- an atmosphere of calm and happiness
- greater tolerance and understanding

Silence is what education needs and has been waiting for. Silence is educational oil. This book discusses the possibility of that idea, by referring to existing work and presenting new evidence and theory.

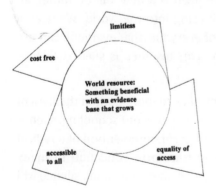

Introduction

Recent work in education has asked: 'At what cost to the individual, to teaching and learning, and to society in general does education ignore the pedagogical value of silence? (Zembylas and Michaelides, 2004:193). This book surveys the field from an introductory perspective, highlighting some work that is going on but also setting markers into the sand. These markers are there to enable navigation of the terrain of theory and practice. Without points of reference it is hard to have the important conversations in education that silence demands. This is especially true in dealing with an idea, a practice and an educational approach which operates without words, without identification even. Having conducted this 'survey', here presented, I absolutely agree with the opening quote of this paragraph: ignoring silence for and in education is a profound pedagogical error. Education needs silence and can benefit from it.

What I mean by 'silence' needs clarification at the outset. Understandably, the strong claim made for silence as beneficial needs to be supported by evidence. I try to answer this by offering a picture of a movement and its reasons, its resources and its dynamics. I present a framework for activity around silence in schools. Next, I offer a perspective. Silence as a practice, an attitude and an experience is freedom. Nothing is to be understood as confining or restricting. I offer markers in the sand that people may interact with and move as they see fit. I do not want to prescribe because silence deserves a higher and more interactive approach, suited to humans in all our wonderful diversity. Silence comes from people and it suits people, but only if it stays free.

What use is silence?

This book focuses on positive silence or what I call 'strong' silence. This is, I consider, a natural silence for people to tune into, to develop, to come towards, that is helpful for living and learning, developing and understanding, interacting and knowing. However, mention of the word 'silence' does not always immediately conjure up such a profile.

When I have mentioned silence in schools to people I meet, certain themes immediately spring out again and again. Firstly, most people have stories of their own about silence and they want to tell them. They tell of childhood dinner tables without conversation; families that did not know how to communicate emotions such as love or anger, so silence had to say it all. They speak of Victorian schoolchildren and shudder at the thought of strictly obeying the teacher's command to be quiet as a mouse. They think mostly of noiselessness and an absence of aural content. Literal silence.

Secondly, most people have a deep relationship to silence that they have rarely questioned. They say it is a very interesting topic. They begin to talk about it and then stumble: do they mean this or that? Their pondering tends not to get far beyond the idea of silence as difficult or negative in some way and as meaning an aural quiet. There is a reason for this. Silence as a topic of *conversation* is akin to a specialist art. How to talk about what is not in or of language? How to know something that cannot be seen or touched? How to understand an absence? Or develop a total lack? Complaining about the negative effects of silence is possible and perhaps easy. But can we engage with silence that is positive? How?

What I hope to do in this book is offer a practical way forward for the use of positive silence in schools by providing conceptual tools by which to grasp this nothingness. I reveal how powerfully silence is a tangible something and I show that silence in schools can attain the status of an improvement, or change practice for schools. At the heart of this book is the idea, shared by many, that silence is positive. I suggest that positive silence might be *necessary* for school education. But if not positive, silence has no place in a school; schools have for too long lived with negative silence without understanding its effects. Education has not yet properly understood why negative, 'weak' silence is anti-educational and detrimental to well-being or why positive, 'strong' forms of silence have a valuable place in schooling.

My argument begins with the practice. Chapter two presents testimonies by four headteachers who work in schools using positive silence as an everyday feature of the educational provision. These are schools that are used to such silence. Staff and students have substantial experience of what it is, how it functions, what it does, why they like it and would not like to be without it. They are important testimonies for teachers who want to know what it is like to be in a school with a whole school ethos for silence practices. The practices they describe may use techniques such as sitting for meditation with a mantra and mindfulness awareness, or they may simply be about sitting or pausing before, after or during activity. Overall, whether the school is using techniqued silence or technique-less silence is shown to be without divisions: all silence blends together into an experience that is particular. Silences that bring benefits pervade these schools in various ways and the stories of practice illustrate this. The experience of silence has left these educationists and their schools in no doubt that elected and carefully tended silences are good for schooling. Reading the testimonies of this awareness is interesting and surprising for educators.

The third chapter considers how teachers who are working in schools that do not have a whole school ethos of silence nonetheless work with positive, strong silence. The two testimonies from practitioners discussed in this chapter come from teachers who have recognised such silence as functioning in special ways in their classrooms. One works in depth with a silence technique of mindfulness and the other has worked for many years with silence without technique. They represent, in small measure, vast numbers of examples in schools where individual teachers have discovered or are discovering what silence can offer their classrooms, their teaching practice and, crucially, their students.

In the fourth chapter I do the job of theorist and place my own markers. In the context of what active, experienced silence practitioners say about positive silence as a part of education, the chapter creates a conceptual framework for a broad understanding of silence in schools. This has to take account of how schools function in a sociological and historical context and not just with reference to the special environments of the schools with substantial experience of what silence can do.

I introduce a bifurcation in a general concept of silence as it works in schools, through naming it as either weak or strong. Silence that is negative in effect and experience is called 'weak'. This is to foster a wide understanding of all and any silence in schools that it ought to be positive. The positive kind I call 'strong' because it is strong enough to deliver and offer benefits. Whilst it might be enough to talk simply about negative and positive silence, in this chapter I argue for why an imposition of some kind of substantial characterising nomenclature upon silence in schools is useful. However, once I have placed some identification markers in the silent, shifting terrain of the topic of silence in schools, I withdraw the differing nomenclature of identification. Thereafter silence is simply referring to the strong form and character is only specified with 'weak' or 'strong' when it is necessary to avoid confusion. It can be assumed that any talk of silence without specification is about the strong kind.

In chapter five an overview is offered of a burgeoning movement of research and school-based activity incorporating (strong) silence. Such silence is becoming fashionable for education and is also proving itself to be important through its reference to research-based evidence conceiving silence practices as effective and useful. The vast array of practices and interested parties is outlined as it is currently understood, with the UK provided as a case study of an international field of activity. Whilst silence is often interpersonally culturally defined and determined, I suggest that silence as educational is common to schooling everywhere, when strong.

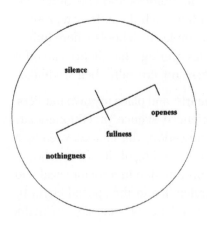

Chapter six offers further investigation about what all this activity might mean for school education. I look at the ways in which silence opens education up to new ways of doing things and of thinking. In particular I argue that silence in schools has the perhaps surprising but powerful ability to make schools function more democratically. It also offers a way for children to appreciate their own natural inner resources in a world of mainly media-driven externalising tendencies of the self.

Chapter seven, the concluding chapter, is deliberately brief and to the point, highlighting what is most important about silence in schools.

Throughout the book, I place diagrams relating to silence as a form of visual topography. Sometimes these are contextualised by the text; sometimes they float within the text, silently.

This book is ...

This is a book about silence. It is not a book about meditation and how to meditate. Nor is it about mindfulness. References to these practices tend to be subsumed under a general term of 'silence practices' and are not discussed here in technical depth. Other people do that well (eg. Nataraja, 2008; Kabat-Zinn, 2005). There are also now overviews of related academic research which offer in-depth analysis outside the remit of this book (eg. Baer, 2003; Burke, 2010). However, meditative practices of all sorts are important to 'silence in schools'. A brief clarification of terms: meditation is a concentration-based approach which 'train[s] participants to restrict the focus of attention to a single stimulus' (Baer, 2003:126), whereas mindfulness is about forms of awareness enhancement, involving 'observation of constantly changing internal and external stimuli as they arise' (*ibid*). There are many types of these two techniqued silences, and understanding the differences is part of the current growing field of research.

These practices are a fundamental part of the richness of the picture of silence in schools. Meditative practices that involve a technique are currently gaining in currency for schooling, as I discuss in chapter five. I provide a context for discussion of meditation and mindfulness as involved in silence in schools, especially from an organisational and theoretical perspective. To focus on meditation and mindfulness in schools more than I do would however, be a different kind of book which would take the focus away from discussion of silence and into other areas such as neuroscience. This book is about silence itself in schools as a phenomenon. It asks:

- What is silence in the context of school education?

- How is silence already used in schools?

- How can appreciation of silence and an introduction of silence into education be helpful, why would it be helpful and for whom?

- Do educationists need to care about silence: is it important for them, us, others and for the various kinds of education they, we believe in?

Meditation and mindfulness play a vital part in this discussion but tend to be in the background of this book, as integral and often initially taught introductions that are techniqued practices of the silence I discuss.

Given the vast literature on silence and the wide ranging uses of silence in schools (see chapters two, three and five), it is surprising that there is not already a wealth of monographic literature outlining what is important about positive, strong silence in schools, accessible beyond journal articles. This is not the case, although a few key books on such silence and aspects of education have emerged in recent years. Along with growing wider social interest in silence, this field in education is developing quickly. Amongst monographs dedicated to exploring silence as a positive function is a book by Schultz focusing mainly on silence in classrooms. It looks at silence in relation to teacher-student participation and 'ways to make silence an affirmative part of the classroom dynamic' (2009:144). A book by Reda is a qualitative pedagogic study of one classroom and of how the students perceive and use silence and how silence can be reconceived by and for students as positive (2009). A Swedish language book by Alerby also focuses on positive silence in education from a number of angles (2012).

To write on silence as a topic is to be faced with myriad choices about direction and focus. There is much excellent work, therefore, that has fallen just outside of my own choices when deciding what to say. If all the possible angles available as presentations are taken into account, the field of 'silence studies' for education is substantial. My own referencing therefore must be selective and even imposes at times a pressure about what I want to say and how, so that many voices do not drown out the silence I am aiming to point at.

Despite a wide range of literature, we are also right at the beginning of exploration of this topic in the mainstream. For instance, discussion of meditative techniques in schools is in its 'infancy' (Burke, 2010; Garrison Institute, 2008). Already though, a swell of mainstream interest in silence for areas connected to spirituality, holism, noise pollution, health, well-being, neuroscience, and so on, sets a tone. All are focusing closely on silence as a topic of importance. This looks set to continue (Hastings and Singh, 2010), due perhaps to the rise of scientific research into the practical benefits of meditative silence practices for all (eg. Harrison *et al*, 2004; Williams *et al*, 2007; Gold *et al*, 2009; Huppert and Johnson, 2010; Semple *et al*, 2010; Burke, 2010).

Silence about silence in schools

While working on this book I was astonished by the extent to which silence, both negative and positive, has been the topic of so many publications in many disciplinary areas, from music to religion to linguistics. But the picture in education is not so broad. Conversations and debate about silence in schools mostly relate to negative, weak silence. Such silence is an historically embedded part of the conduct of school learning and behaviour: telling/compelling children to be quiet (rather than asking them to take account of others) or imposing silent line-ups outside classrooms or silent assemblies or silent work as punishment or ignoring homosexual or sexist bullying as a silence. These are all familiar schooling matters and fairly well documented (eg. Walkerdine, 1985; Leander, 2002) so that it is possible to identify how weak silence is playing an active role in schools. From an educational studies and practice perspective, there is however, too much silence in schools and education about positive strong silence.

Strong silence and its positive practices have until recently been largely ignored as a fundamental part of education activity in schools. The research that does exist about forms of strong silence in schools has not entered into the consciousness of school practitioners to the extent that most teachers are aware of how silence can function as a pedagogic tool in their classrooms. Nor, it seems, are teachers yet fully aware of some of their classroom control practices as overtly connected to silence in negative ways, despite the substantial literature on weak silence. People take silence for granted and do not, it seems, engage in theory about what silence is and can do as a *something*. It would appear that schools have been functioning so far with scant regard for what I and the other writers on silence in education consider is an important element for and of educational practice. Whether weak or strong, silence has power. Brought into consciousness it becomes an educational feature. Disregarded, it still has power but not necessarily in helpful ways because it colludes with features of schooling that operate beneath the surface (see eg. Bowles and Gintis, 1976).

Two articles in particular serve as counter examples to a lack of awareness and take silence into the realm of the positive and as strong enough to deliver benefit to classrooms. Ros Ollin shows how certain teachers have given silence deep thought. She provides an interesting list of forms of silence that function in classrooms, according to teachers she interviewed, which range in practice from ways of standing in a particular space to even leaving a room altogether (Ollin, 2008). Some of these ideas are discussed in chapter five as methods for the introduction of silence into schools. Adam Jaworski did research in the classroom, asking children how they saw silence as a something functioning in their schools (Jaworski, 1993). What is missing so far from the literature on positive silence is a wide overview of theory and practice from different perspectives, which can provide a framework and introduction to debates and practice for school education. I try to present this here as part of a conversation which responds to what we already know, and which can be taken up and continued.

Since school education is seen globally as so important (Alexander, 2009; Ramirez and Boli, 1987; Tooley, 2009), to have a situation where a hegemonic and pervading human concept such as silence is literally silenced in education is weird.

So whilst the world is not short of discussions on silence, and silence as a topic is no longer marginal (Jaworski, 1997), discussions of beneficial silence in the context of education and educational research are still relatively few. This is incommensurate with the importance of the field of education, the significance of silence in human lives and therefore the possible impact of the two areas when brought together. An active role for positive strong silence in school contexts is only just emerging in the mainstream. With it comes a burgeoning literature on 'contemplative pedagogy' (eg. Orr, 2002; Brady, 2007; Garrison Institute, 2008). But some schools have been using silence for decades and testimonies of this experience are a part of this book. The history of silence is greater and longer than our concept of education. Just as we have much to learn from education about silence, we also have much to learn from silence for education.

Silence in the discipline of disciplines of education

Dauenhauer identifies silence as having specific characteristics according to the specific discipline: politics, religion, art, technology. All have different characteristic silences which conjoin with their disciplinary area to provide a background and specific functions of opening and closing of silence (Dauenhauer, 1980:26-49). Furthermore, the silence of each discipline can silence that of another. For instance, the awed silence of a religious service needs to cease before a different kind of silence can begin, such as the silence of the impersonal elements that come with scientific study. Political discourse has a silence of reverence for the founders of the political world in which it operates. Artistic silence is about the generation of the challenging or the refreshing of understandings, whilst technological silences involve both a passive use of technology and ambitious visions of its uses.

What these distinctions offer us is the possibility and even the likelihood that silence in schools, as an aspect of education in general, has a silence of its own which can be philosophically and perhaps empirically identified. By identifying a silence characteristic of education – if this is possible when we are not sure what education is or can be (Condliffe Lagemann, 2002; Labaree, 2006; Sidorkin, 2011) – can the use of silence in schools be better understood? If there is a silence particular to schools and it is not political or religious or artistic or any other kind, is it 'educational' silence or a type of silence of schools as institutions? In a context of education as constructed: comprised by various disciplines of philosophy, history, psychology, sociology, economics, geography (see Lawn and Furlong, 2011), as variously constituted according to national history, culture and language (Biesta, 2011), or plain inter-disciplinary in nature, to what extent are these perspectives and constructions *undone* by silence in education? Could silence as an actively recognised positive principle of education challenge what education is 'itself'? (Moran, 2012). How does silence make and unmake education? This book ponders these questions.

In conclusion

This book points towards a new arena for serious exploration in education. It indirectly poses a meta-question that reaches beyond school-age into what it might mean to lead a healthy and fruitful life:

> If children, starting at a young age and continuing throughout their school years, were able to experience stillness and silent activities during the school day, might they be better equipped to draw on the benefits that silence and solitude offer? (Haskins, 2010:2)

The responses to this question are complex. But, as this book relates, silence is shown, here and also through peer-reviewed scientifically oriented research, to be of importance for physical health and well-being. And it is potentially of profound significance for a new approach to educational practice that offers a redemption of schooling systems in trouble.

The evidence and discussion builds a picture of education as connected to a new tool. This tool is unusual in both its ordinariness and its special nature. Silence is beautiful once achieved or received. The research literature is replete with testimonies to this effect from children and staff. Those who have practiced with it, who speak directly in this book, say this also. Possibly the greatest beauty of it, though, is that it is already in place in schools, already paid for, as soon as people walk through the door. It appears to be an inbuilt natural, effective, enjoyable and beneficial, non coercive technology for a better education.

The book presents case studies of specific and real practices of (strong) silence in schools from conversations with the school-based educationists involved. All are based in the UK. These schools are not named in the course of the discussion. Along with an overview of the research methodology given in the Appendix is a list of some key schools whose practice is with silence, established as a long-standing feature of the school ethos and of practice with the children and staff. By not directly identifying the individuals and schools interviewed whose practice has vitally enhanced the understanding of (strong) school silence that this book offers, I hope that a helpful effect can emerge for all schools.

Currently most schools with a sustained interest in silence are fee-paying but this is irrelevant. Through the anonymity, I wish to under-line that the interviewees are not suggesting direction for other schools of a similar or different type but are talking purely about their own experiences. Silence in schools can be accessible to all to develop according to their own institutional, philosophic, social and practical backgrounds. Silence is organic practice. As we will see, wherever and however it happens, it is part of a journey of some kind.

The writing of this book has been a tremendous pleasure but has also seemed at times a heavy responsibility. The communities of practi-tioners of silence in its many forms expect and need greater dissemina-tion of their practices. It is right that this should happen in and for realms where children congregate. But the book is only a small contri-bution to such important, exciting and growing work. *Such* attention is now, rightly, being paid by many people to silence and its practices, as an elixir of hope for education and in the lives of children. No one author responds to this astonishing emergence on their own and this is why I find silence so utterly intriguing and full, to my mind, of 'seculari-sable spirituality': it is *truly* democratic. It takes us into the arena of all our selves where no one voice is sufficient or complete, thereby opening up a person's heart to the self and voice of others. Whilst we may speak, what we say can never communicate better than the voice of silence and this can be humbling. Perhaps true democracy and true education are wordless. Whether either exist; whether either are possible in and from silence, is explored here. Both words and silence are used in the discussion.

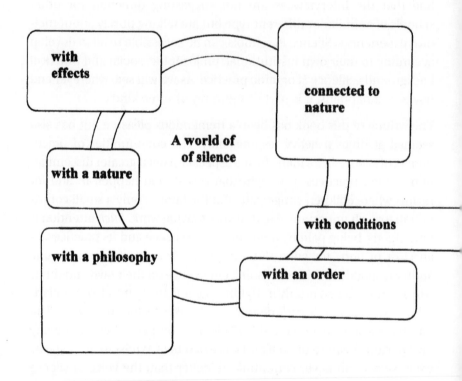

with
effects

connected to
nature

A world of
of silence

with a nature

with conditions

with a philosophy

with an order

1

What is silence?

The mercurial nature of silence

The nature of silence is beautifully unruly. It is rebellious and free of capture, so pinning it down in epistemological terms is not always appropriate. According to Dauenhauer (1980), it functions as the significant space between; a lever to apply pressure; a key to open locks on new rooms of meaning and an elevator to other levels of discourse. Silence moves and takes with it meaning; it is a form of transit; a translator 'from the known to the unknown' (Caranfa, 2004:218). We must recognise that how we talk about silence depends 'on the theoretical frameworks and methodologies adopted for its study' (Jaworski and Sachdev, 1998:274). As a moving, shifting target it is also coloured variously by perspectives when it gets talked about.

In addition to its mercurial flight and flexibility, silence as a topic has the nature of radicality and revolution, as I discuss later. So it would be foolish to suggest what silence is, without simultaneously suggesting that silence refuses the imposition of definition. What we make of silence becomes entirely our own, not determined by another person. Perhaps no other topic is so open to these possibilities. This sounds like an author's nightmare but what it means, and which is in fact helpful, is that silence as a topic belongs to all of us equally. A writer on silence knows at heart no more or less than a person who experiences silence. What we make of it we make of it ourselves. It is not a topic that gets dictated to us by another voice. This creates a situation where dialogue (ironically) is especially suited to this topic however difficult articulation might be. Despite, or because of such difficulties, I have sought to make this presentation as practical and accessible as I can, and to not lose the precious topic of silence in its own nature as it is too valuable. Silence offers the following:

- independence

- radicality

- freedom of thought and expression

- facilitating inter-personal dialogue; not monologic dictation

Silence may be mercurial as itself, but (strong) silence in schools is also a solid topic to consider. Because it is alive and free as a topic, it is an exciting arena for practice and theory. As a subject matter for discussion it can escape to realms outside of language, if a shift is made to ways of thinking that are not determined and constructed by language. When this happens it can feel good: like a realisation. Despite the 'slippery' nature of silence (Schwartz, 1996) into and out of relation to language, it is possible to work with it and approach it in meaningful ways through talking about it.

Whatever the difficulties, we need to talk about silence in schools and for education. Ollin calls such talk about silence "meta-silence', where the teacher deliberately teaches or discusses silence and the processes of silence' (2008:274). She suggests it '... could be important for teachers to consider this as an integral part of their communicative repertoire.' (*ibid*). She also notes in her study that '... silences were often misunderstood and undervalued ...' (p277). Amongst those who do think about silences there is an awareness of a lack of understanding and value for silence amongst those who do not think about them. Consequently, the more talk we have about silence, the more we will be able to understand it and know why it might be valued. The irony of the situation spawns jokes along a similar theme of 'what will you talk about?'.

Defining silence for the sake of talk

To approach silence as a topic in a practical fashion for discussion, we need to define what is meant here by 'silence'. As Glenn says 'Like the zero in mathematics, silence is an absence with a function ...' (2004:4). Determining a definition of this 'absence' helps us to understand function.

The task brings numerous possibilities and difficulties to bear on our understanding because of the complexity of the concept (Jaworski, 1993; Tannen and Saville-Troike, 1995), but complexity need not be a problem. There are many levels on which to talk about a definition of silence and silences. There is an opportunity for depth of understanding but it is also a way to get lost.

Silence is a vast subject, incorporating many domains: art, religion, linguistics, psychology and others. Writings discussing it as phenomenon, salve, friend, philosophy, outcome, aim, problem, saviour, God, terror, torment, denial and so on, are easy to find. Silence is everywhere; all things to all people. This is perhaps surprising, given that modern writing advocating silence suggests the world has lost touch with its presence (eg. see Maitland, 2008; Sim, 2007; Hempton and Grossman, 2009; Prochnik, 2010). The word 'silence' appears with astonishing frequency. Writing about noise, there it is; writing about quiet, there it is; writing about people, there it is; writing about animals, there too. It is never far from being used. Silence is so multi-natured it is helpful in a huge variety of contexts and in linguistic terms is a pliable word, linked to intricate networks of different signifiers. Jaworski discusses it as 'a diverse concept' and 'wide-ranging' (1997:3). Although it would be a construction, creating a concept of silence in education helps us talk about its effects on school education.

People I spoke to in school education seem instinctively to see silence as being of two different types. They use their own terms: good or bad, positive or negative, for instance. Bruneau (1973) uses a bifurcation of 'slow time' and 'fast time' to indicate types of experience, with 'slow time' corresponding in some ways in spirit to what I call 'strong silence'. In work that is unconnected to education, my strong silence is named as 'deep silence' (Dauenhauer, 1980). It is seen as occurring in 'many modes ... namely, the silence of intimates, liturgical silence, and the silence of the to-be-said' (pp16-17).

For Dauenhauer there is 'the absence of a necessary conjunction between deep silence and any particular determinate utterance' (p17). In other words there is no need to speak and speech is not present. My own definition of (strong) silence is in tune with this (see chapter four). What I would add is that such a silence can never be *known*, although

3

knowing this is to recognise a relationship to and even with it. Silence is unknowable and this has implications for silence in schools. Knowing this means one has begun to know its nature in some way: a journey of recognition has begun. An inability to grasp silence as knowledge is to face it with humility for the Other (Zembylas and Michaelides, 2004). There are numerous difficulties in knowing silence as 'defined' and chief amongst them is the dance of the binary.

A lack of a binary

Despite my imposed bifurcation on silence as weak and strong for the management of the concept in education, I suggest in chapters four and six that silence, particularly in schools, is not part of a binary. Silence is not an absence of noise or a state of audible quiet; it is not in contra-distinction with something. There must be no binary in the domain of strong silence. Weak silence can tolerate a binary and it may need one to do its damage: telling children to be silent against their will demands the concept of noise versus quiet.

It is important to pay attention to this when we consider silence in a context of school education. Schools are possibly the most dualistically saturated institution ever: right and wrong, good and bad, quiet and loud, clever and not clever, academic and vocational, strict and easy going, hard and easy, worthwhile and pointless, obedient and disobedient, hard working and lazy, etc. School settings function according to duality so they can order their work, signify their meanings publically and fit into a framework of the world that can connect to what schools do, without ambiguity. Silence in schools that does not pertain to duality in easily understandable ways is a concept of change when it is present. It is a fundamental and radical intervention into schooling, which quite literally makes a difference. It escapes the known.

A state of mind

Silence is scientifically testable and quantifiable. Alpha wave states, which can be measured, are a product of the mind being able to coalesce its energies in a harmonious manner known as 'hypersynchrony', in response to a meditative state emerging in both hemispheres of the brain (Mann, 2001). Seigel (2006) chooses to define the mind as 'an embodied process that regulates the flow of energy and information'. Silence practices used in ways which strengthen the mind by regulating this flow towards hypersynchronious states of peace and calm, are a technique for creating mind states which are silent by nature (Siegel, 2010). They use the natural resources of the body to create silence. The mind has been strengthened or is strengthening itself to be in a state of quietude that results from harmony. Such harmony might also occur by means of a mental shift from the left hemisphere of the brain, where busy rumination is processed, to the calmer right side (Bolte Taylor, 2008).

Silence as meant here is present in educational contexts as a state of mind. This could be termed also a mood or feeling but is a literal state of mind that is physiological. As a state of mind relying on flow, it is likely to be incrementally achieved and built upon because practice at managing the flow matters (see eg. Huppert and Johnson, 2010).

Bruneau claims that 'silence appears to be a concept and process of mind which is imposed by each mind on itself and on the minds of others' (1973:17). Silence as a state of mind can be a specific concept of an 'experience' of consciousness. Scientifically, this can be seen thus:

> As the brain becomes activated in the moment, it coalesces its firing patterns into clusters of activation we can call a 'state of mind.' These repeated and enduring states of activation of the brain can help define what we see as our personality, our patterns of perception and emotional and behavioral responses that help us denote who we are. (Siegel, 2006:12)

Combining ideas of unknowing, consciousness and physical states, this 'state of mind' of (strong) silence is a physical embodiment of neuronal activity that develops a sense and experience of quietude. This creates an individual experience of silence as a tangible and communal experience which begins to challenge a solely scientific perspective as sufficient without other ways of seeing what silence is being also available.

Lisa A. Mazzei says in *Inhabited Silence in Qualitative Research*, 'Silence can never receive a 'hearing' if voiced speech is the measure of what is credible' (2007:4). To understand the credible we need community. We also need a different perspective on silence from that which we apply to speech. Indeed we require another framework of approach to understanding it altogether when it is experienced. Jiddu Krishnamurti identifies this difference:

5

It is not a silence which the observer can experience. If he does experience it and recognise it, it is no longer silence. The silence of the meditative mind is not within the borders of recognition, for this silence has no frontier. There is only silence – in which the space of division ceases. (Krishnamurti, 1970)

This 'experience' imbued with calm, joy, a sense of wholeness and an appreciation of the world is not constructed out of parts because the idea of division no longer exists in the mind. It is a holistic silence as a state of mind or a 'mindset' (Garrison Institute, 2008:3) that is 'kept' whereby '... silences are intentionally produced states of persons', closely connected to a sense of or actual stillness of the body (Cooper, 2008; Cooper, 2012).

Silence as 'kept' is part of my understanding of how silence can come about. However, bodily stillness is not necessarily a profound part of silence for children and staff in schools. The 'state of mind' of kept silence is a sense of flow (Csikszentmihalyi, 2008) that can be used as a form of metonymic 'stillness'. It is mental rather than physical. Although physical stillness can greatly help mental stillness to occur, it is not the determining factor. In this state of mind, the mind is not ruminating widely and without control. Instead it is concentrated on its task, be it running after a ball or sitting immobile, focusing on a thought; becoming more aware of what is occurring in the present. The idea of such a mind-state with movement is found in techniqued elite physical expression in sport, where athletes or players get into 'the zone' (Lardon, 2008). But techniqued silence in schools is usually a meditative practice with no movement, eyes often closed to block out distractions; moving towards a state of mind.

This state of mind as silent is a negation of dualistic ideas and their realities. It emerges partly from the physical fact that a mind attuned by silence practices (see chapter five) is coherent:

> People who come to develop the capacity to pay attention in the present moment without grasping on to their inevitable judgments also develop a deeper sense of well-being and what can be considered *a form of mental coherence*. (Siegel, 2006:4 emphasis added)

This coherence is formed by the left and right sides of the brain working in tune, rather than dysfunctionally or antagonistically (Siegel, 2010). Silence and its silence practices facilitate the emergence of this coherence, helping the mind-brain to be more 'co-operative' and less divided in terms of a conflict of left and right hemispheres (see McGilchrist, 2009). Although coherence – a coming together – can also occur spontaneously and even repeatedly without prior technical meditative practices, as part of everyday experiences: triggers of the everyday such as meeting a new person can cause enhanced experience, bordering even on the mystical (eg. see Laski, 1980; Dewey, 1960). Silence of coherence is a lack of conflict, a merging. It is a natural part of human existence but is a state of mind that can come and go. Regular silence practices could be said to feed its maintenance, sustain and inform its power in practical, neurological ways.

But silence as a state of mind is more than neurobiological facts. It is an inner realisation. Being beyond dualism it is positive and whole. It resides, dwells, abides and a person realises their part in that by coming upon this silence state of mind. The headteachers interviewed in chapter two indicate that residing, dwelling, abiding silence is, however, not a given. It is conditionally present and experienced; generous in access but asking for respect and attention.

The definition I present of silence as a non-dualistic state of mind refers to its positive self: silence that is not this positive 'self' is not silence but instead something else that gets called 'silence'. It is an impostor, a form of mental noise.

When the silence discussed in this book is in operation it is a space, a place, a feeling, an experience. It is *not* an absence of sound. Noise levels have little to do with the silence discussed here, although it is helped by an absence of invasive aural distraction. Sounds themselves can be silent in the sense I mean:

> To experience the soul-swelling wonder of silence you must hear it. Silence is a sound, many many sounds. I've heard more than I can count. Silence is the moonlit song of the coyote signing the air, and the answer of its mate. It is the falling whisper of snow that will later melt with an astonishing reggae rhythm that you will want to dance to ... It is the sound of pollinating winged insects ... (Hempton and Grossman, 2009:3)

A silent state of mind is most at ease within a physical environment which has silent features, where silence is meant in an auditory sense. A minimum of noise is conducive to silence in schools.

7

So 'silence' as used in this book goes against the grain of what people might regularly or commonly understand from it as having a connection to noise. The hegemonic sense of the word 'silence' is naturally noiselessness – but noiselessness does not exist. Whilst quests are made for perfect silence (eg. Foy, 2010), the world continues to spin and no doubt makes a noise of some kind somewhere whilst it does so. John Cage, the composer famous for his radical 4'33" piece of music in which performers sit silently for four minutes and thirty three seconds, entered an anechoic (soundproofed and sound absorbent) chamber at Harvard University. He discovered that in this carefully designed and scientifically measured silent space he continued to hear two subtle but constant sounds. On leaving the chamber he was told that the high pitched noise he had noticed was his nervous system and the lower pitched noise was his blood pumping through his body. For Cage this meant that 'we need not fear about the future of music' (Cage, 1961:8), suggesting that noise (or the noises humans make as various forms of music) will never leave us because 'try as we may to make a silence, we cannot' (*ibid*). But we can make music that works with and approaches a silent state of mind.

In a similar vein, school settings accommodate children who are naturally talented at making noise of various kinds. This means that however 'silent' in the dualistic 'noise/not noise' sense of the word a school gets, the future of the noise of children or of a school with noise in it, is not in question. Noiseless settings are a human impossibility. Yet school settings that approach and work with silence as a value are not impossible and when they do that work, they seem to quieten down (Farrer, 2000).

I define silence as necessarily undefinable; a state of mind that is created by experiences of many kinds. It involves a sense of well-being that does not need to be discussed, once achieved. Such silence is a gift.

Chapter two explores the most important aspect of silence: the views of school practitioners who work with silence every day.

2

Whole school experiences
of silence

UK3: Silence is the critical unifying factor.

UK1: That common unifying essence of everybody ... It's very unifying because everybody is doing it.

UK4: ... it's about community. It's about silence with everybody.

UK2: ... the school has grown over a number of years in a certain quality and ... as a whole community.

Introduction

The silence in schools explored here is a strong presence, a strong experience, a silence strong enough to bring forth benefits. Until we hear about what this means in practice it remains puzzling, but hearing testimonies of what it is like to work with strong silence in schools is illuminating. Testimonies from experienced practitioners fill in some of the natural silences about this topic and they also offer access to knowledge of how strong silence works in practice. People sharing their understanding of working with it in school settings can tell other educationists who might want to use silence actively, what outcomes they might expect and what needs to be taken into consideration. The quotes by the headteachers interviewed in this chapter illustrate the function of silence in strengthening a sense of community in the schools. Philosopher John MacMurray, who talked about 'real education' (see Stern, 2001), would see it as a sign of educational success because a school's:

9

... first principle is that it must be a real community. Not because community is a good thing – I would underline this – but because this is the condition of success in its educational function. (Macmurray, 1968, in Stern, 2001:31-32)

This chapter presents discussions with headteachers who have long experience of silence in schools as an integral part of the daily education of students and the staff's working environment. I have placed these conversations early in the book because the burgeoning movement of silence in schools is still so new. They portray the idea or concept of silence in schools as it manifests in practice, in a working context.

The headteachers speaking in this chapter are involved with schools that have worked with silence for many years and have a tradition of silence. They are experienced guides to silence as a part of schooling. As far as I am aware, this is the first time they have been asked as part of a study about how strong silence works and what it does for their schools.

I have anonymised the participants not so much to conceal their identity but because what happens in their schools with silence is not specific to them. Their schools are all free from the National Curriculum and this has allowed other philosophies of education to be explored. But their whole school ethos of silence can certainly be replicated elsewhere. However, translation from one type of school to another, one place to another and from one community of people to another, as the following testimonies suggest, is complicated by the conditions of silence in schools. These emerge in the interview conversations and are summarised in the conclusion.

All schools can be with silence, just as all people have recourse to silence. The degree of integration of silence in a school depends on the number of people interested to work with it, the guiding principles of the school and a willingness to believe it has value for education.

The interviews with headteachers

It became apparent in the discussions that each school had a profound relationship to silence. Silence was important for the schools as an aspect of the educational provision they offered. Each person who speaks here has experience of silence in their own personal lives and all found silence deeply interesting. This is a common feature of working with it: the more one grows to understand how it works, the more it opens itself up for reflection and discovery. They described silence as a substance, as thing, as character, almost as a person in the room. This is not unusual in the literature on silence. Max Picard (2002) considers silence to be a 'world' and therefore tangible. Anne Le Clair (2009), in her regular submission to days of total silence, saw it as a friend. Kenny observes that 'silence sometimes assumes the qualities of a presence ...' (Kenny, 2011:67).

The methodology for the conduct of these interviews is provided in the appendix. The testimonies in this chapter are referred to as UK1-4.

Silence as a presence in schools

The first quotes reflect the idea of silence in a school setting as a presence:

> **UK1**: It's a sharing. Everybody is in that same substance. I must say that the silence is there all the time. Whatever it is, that substance, energy, stillness, whatever.
>
> **HL**: What do you mean by substance?
>
> **UK1**: Good question. It's something tangible.
>
> **UK4**: I think the silence, I think what the silence does is it's very, very grounding. So after you've done it you actually look for it. You know, the girls actively enjoy it. And as they get older and older they value it more and more and more and more and more. And even the younger ones know, even though it's a bit fidgety, it's a bit hard to do, there's something in them that knows that inherently, it's a value.
>
> **HL**: You are using the word 'it' lots of times.
>
> **UK4**: Silence, yes.
>
> **HL**: Yeh no, okay so the 'it' is the silence?
>
> **UK4**: Yes.
>
> **HL**: But in other places, teachers have been talking about silence as an 'it'. So they've been suggesting that it is something.
>
> **UK4**: Oh I see, yes.
>
> **HL**: Do you, have you come ... have you ever thought that silence is not just a sort of, a vague notion or a ...
>
> **UK4**: Oh no, yes it's, silence is definitely something.

When silence in a school functions on a regular basis, a benign atmosphere steadily builds up:

UK1: New parents recognise the atmosphere. I would say that's related to these common principles, this access to stillness, they think it's happy ... talking about silence it sounds like it's quiet all the time, but it's not! (laughs heartily) ... [It] alters the atmosphere and the effect is cumulative.

UK2: I suppose that this whole area of meditation and silence is actually very subtle in what it accesses, what it touches. Um, I can't explain why, but I think that what it does is water and open up an essential sweetness which is at the core of being and I suppose in that respect it probably serves to dissolve other stuff. You don't control that but it just kinda happens. You know it's like that when you walk into any place where people have been meditating, there is a great sweetness there in the atmosphere.

UK3: So we offer to the boys ten minutes of what we call quiet time in the mornings and ten minutes of quiet time in the afternoons before the afternoon begins and we also offer a sense of pausing and stopping for about half a minute or so and an emptying of the mind at the end and beginning of every activity and the beginning and end of every lesson. So it builds up a platform of responsiveness and confidence really, which is important for a boy so that he can begin something afresh and I would say that there are two main methods of working in this way.

One is in terms of – if you like – a secular approach to education which is just in terms of the facility to attend. The biggest educational challenge most teachers face is getting the boys' attention. Game-boys and excessive exposure to computers and all that stuff ... it is very difficult on their powers of concentration and attention. We notice it on Monday mornings. Monday mornings it takes us about two hours to get anywhere near learning, having spent the weekend on their game-boys and video machines. As the week unfolds and they're getting these practices it gets better and better so just educationally it's very, very useful. Spiritually it has another impact ...

UK4: So for me, I think ... I think the silence that you've just witnessed gives the school ... an air of calm. So it is a calm place but it's very purposeful. So when you go on a tour a little bit later on, it's very alive ... So at break times, lunchtimes, we give the girls, the children, freedom. So they've got freedom to play outside, work, do whatever they want to do. And it is lovely to see that in their free time, they use it. They don't just huddle and chat. There's a sense of, they play or they work, or they meet with staff in an area of the school where there are newspapers. And very often if you walk past that at break times, lunchtimes, staff sit there with girls and do crosswords. And so there's a real sense of purpose and ... energy. And I think you were talking a little bit about that with [the deputy headteacher] about how, what energy the silence brings.

The creation of psychological space

What silence seems to be able to offer a school is the creation of psychological space, which in turn offers the possibility for inter-personal tolerance and harmony. Educationists writing about silence describe its ability to become a 'creative and nourishing space' (Kenny, 2011:67). Practitioner researchers remark: 'Into the space carved out by this silence, all manner of understandings have come to me ...' (Brady, 2007:372). The headteachers interviewed often observed how silence develops space within the space of the school:

UK1: It's become absolutely natural [for the children]. You say, let's have a pause.

HL: How do they react when you say that?

UK1: Well, they just do it. I just say listen and as soon as you say it there's this amazing space. They don't just stand there being odd. You just say it and they listen. [After the pause has finished] they'll say amazing things ... surprising things. ... and very, very moving.

UK3: ... Spiritually it has another impact. We ... the boys with us in their quiet times, they can meditate transcendentally if they wish to. They can contemplate. They can practice some breathing exercises drawn from the Buddhist tradition if they wish to. They can just basically sit and be. We only have one rule which is that you do not disturb the peace of another man. Or they can pray. ... the thing that really inspires me is when I look along the row and I see a Muslim boy, a Hindu boy sitting next to him and a Christian boy sitting next to him, a Jewish boy sitting next to him, a boy of no religion and they've all got their eyes closed. They're all in the same space but they're probably all doing something different. So how you get to the stillness doesn't matter in my view.

HL: ... if you're gonna have conversations about it, you're gonna try and work with it and if you notice that it's sort of less than you want and so on, that's a lot of care. That's a lot of attention, and why?

UK4: Because for me as the Head, it comes back to the importance I place on being able to think for yourself. Ultimately silence is a discipline isn't it?

And within that discipline, if we, I'm talking about girls but, you know, if we can ... if the girls can really use that time to really and truly think for themselves, that is so valuable to them as they leave school and go into life. That, as I said to you, for me is the most important thing because hot housing and getting exam results is not enough. And being able to think for yourself, at any point, you know, under pressure or ... and having the confidence too. So being able to stand up! You didn't see that this morning but having the confidence in the gathering to stand up and say what you think.

The question for me is, is education today really allowing children to think for themselves? We're doing a lot of spoon feeding. We're testing all the way. Are we really giving? And also for me, I care because it gives space. It gives a sense of space in our lives, and I care, because of the way that we're living in such a changing world with technology. That's fine, we have to embrace that. But it doesn't give us any space in our lives. And I think it's not because children are just attached to their mobile phones ... So there's no space from that. So that is a little bit of space that I think probably will become more, it will become more sharply focused as the technology moves on.

HL: It's not physical space you're talking about?

UK4: No, the silence gives mental space.

The idea of space frequently features in reports from teachers about silence. Ollin found that teachers she spoke to about their various silence practices, mostly in further education colleges, mentioned 'inter-spaces' for reflection' (Ollin, 2008:270), as 'dream spaces' (*ibid*: 271) for creative thinking and silence spaces as '... allowing students' thoughts to be free from the intrusion of someone else's ideas – teachers and peers – giving them the opportunity to develop ideas for themselves' (*op cit*).

Interpersonal smoothness and lack of friction

Picard speaks about the power of silence to avoid friction: 'The substance of silence stands between the contradictions and prevents them from fighting each other' (Picard, 2002:66). The headteachers remarked upon a sense of space which silence ushers in so that the communal rules of a school can be accepted by the students without too much friction, resistance or alienation. This creates a school environment that flows and functions without hostility, as described here:

UK2: ... the environment can release that and encourage it to find its expression which it does intellectually, creatively, artistically, in all manner of ways according to the particularity of the individual nature and as far as silence is concerned I think that probably allows that process to emerge more cleanly and in a less cluttered way. It gives it space really ...

HL: ... you've got them free at lunchtime and break time. And ... you are encouraging them to think for themselves. And from what you've said I'm putting together the, the space of the silence and the standing up and that sort of training in being confident and so on. That would give ... it creates a sense, for me, of an education which is not coercive.

UK4: That's exactly it because what happens here is the girls want to learn. We have no school rules. So when I say that, yes and obviously if they get it wrong, you know, drugs, alcohol, whatever, then there are, yes we've suspended, do all those kinds of things. But I'm talking about on a day to day basis. You know, 'Helen you've forgotten your pencil, here's an orange mark'. And then on the third day that you've forgotten your pencil and you've got three orange marks, that then translates into a red mark and three red marks translates into a detention. And then the other way round, sort of 'house points'. You've remembered your pencil! And we don't have any of that. And we've, again, talked to the girls about that. They don't want that either. Because what we're saying is: this is your school. We trust you to do, to look after it and be part of this community. And they rise to that challenge.

So we have very, very little low level anything. The only time I have girls in here for, you know, for negative reasons is when they've got it really, really wrong which is very rare. So that isn't to say that the girls here are super human and we don't have issues and fallings out and whatever. But generally speaking, in terms of behaviour you can see it's beautiful, they look after it. Locker areas are terrible and that's fine, that's as it should be because they're children, they are youngsters. But you go to the library which I'm very proud of! Show girls, show people round the library at any time of the day, night, weekday, weekend and it's beautiful! And the girls work in there silently without being told 'be quiet'. They want to do it. So it's a sense of wanting to engage ...

So what I think which is important for girls, is out there you'll see girls up to the age of fifteen, sixteen running around, playing hide and seek and just playing. You wouldn't see that in a co-ed school. So it's that real sense of freedom. Confidence to be yourself. Somebody said to me 'do you want me to ... do you want the girls running round there outside?'. I said 'absolutely I do. I never ever want to tell them to be quiet or not run around'. And if they want to run around in their shoes, with their shoes off, that's okay. They could

15

roll around in the grass, I tell parents that, you know [laughs]. It's all around having this sense of freedom within, within a sort of sense of purpose. Not just freedom to kind of rampage.

But, you know, it is very, very unusual. I've never quite been anywhere where it's been such a stark contrast. And I think they value themselves ...

HL: So when you say stark contrast, that here, there's a contrast between places where you've worked?

UK4: No I just meant the contrast between, you know, actually they have this huge freedom. And yet it's not abused by them. They ... they respect [it].

No harsh edges

Although these schools have established and traditional structures of order and discipline, the integration of silence into their workings means that coercion against the self of students (who may disagree with something) is unnecessary intrusion. A willingness to listen to authority is more in evidence. Also, a willingness for authority to be careful and meaningful (and not arbitrary) is there. This happens in ways that are unusual for school environments functioning through authority and hierarchy. The traditional structures are significantly imbued with thoughtfulness about the effect of these schooling mechanisms for order on the human self:

UK2: I'm very clear about the dos and don'ts at an ordinary human level.

HL: Do you mean right and wrong?

UK2: Well, just codes of conduct that keep things in good order. So for example the girls need to pay proper respect to the teachers, the teachers need to behave professionally, dress professionally. People don't criticise each other, they don't seek to divide each other. It's just these sort of ordinary codes of conduct that are conducive either to unity or harmony and then that's all you have to do. You just get out of the way really.

HL: Could you do that without the silence practices that [your school] likes?

UK2: You could. You could ...

HL: So does it facilitate a way of people being with each other which you notice as specific?

UK2: Yes, and I only recognise that in retrospect. I think – and this has only occurred to me relatively recently – I think what quietude does is it increases, um, a kind of sensitivity – a human sensitivity – which is a lovely thing and I considered how or why that must happen and its partly this fact that as you become quiet, things dissolve. So, what's left is the natural sensitivity of the human apparatus and the human apparatus is sensitive when all the accumulated stuff is let go of – our hearts are sensitive, our minds are sensitive, a bit like a young child is sensitive. There's that but there's also the fact that when you meditate, however you meditate, your powers of observation are heightened ... Your awareness is heightened and that then goes into action in your human engagements, so I think what happens is that people are just more aware of each other more aware of each other's conditions, more aware of the effect of their actions, more careful, kinder.

HL: And from that carefulness and that kindness does care come out?

UK2: Naturally. You don't do that, it just seems to be there.

HL: What happens when you have a group of people together who are heightening their abilities in this regard because of these silence practices-what is the affect of a critical mass of that together?

UK2: Um, well I don't know, it's just a kindly environment. It's gentle. People will say of the girls that they're gentle but they're strong, they have an enormous strength inside. Obviously gentleness, some people might think is weakness, but it isn't. The hard outer edge that people wear isn't strength. The real strength is within. I was going to say that one of the things is that teachers who come here from other schools – one of the things they comment on in quite early days is 'for us it's an experience we've not had before to come into a staffroom and not to get the impression that people have been talking about you and to leave the staffroom and have no question in your mind that they'll talk about you when you've gone'. You know there isn't an atmosphere of back-biting.

Managing silence as an art

There is an art to the management of silence. It demands engagement and practice:

HL: But in this school how do you manage it?

UK4: What do you mean? I'm not sure I'm clear as to what do you mean by 'manage it'.

HL: Well if you've got, there's [many of this particular kind of] schools and they're all different. Is there ... is the way that the silence happens the same in all of the schools? So you mentioned okay clearly there's, I'm assuming there's a meeting for worship in all of the schools. But you are talking about

17

silence at the beginning of staff meetings. And you suggested that some-times there might be silence in lessons.

UK4: Oh I see, yes. I think that moves and grows. Yes, how do I manage it? I manage it by one of the [foundational philosophical underpinning] principles is really including everybody in the conversation and talking to people. So it's about ... it's about seeing what's here. So one of the things, one of the things I did is we didn't have silence before a staff meeting when I arrived. And I said 'let's try and do that'. And it's about ... there was the feeling that our meetings, our morning meetings were not as grounded as they could have been. So we thought 'how are we going to make that even better?'

Now in other schools, in the middle of a meal a bell is rung and everybody has a, a silence and [it] doesn't matter whether you are in the beginning, middle or end of your meal, there's that silence. That used to happen here, it doesn't happen anymore. So there are lots of little ... so that's a silence in another school that we don't have. So it's about, it's about sort of putting in what you, what you feel works for your own school because [the particular foundational philosophical underpinning] isn't, you know, it's not rigid.

HL: So in those conversations then, the two that you mentioned about, 'let's have silence at the beginning of the staff meeting', and 'the meeting for wor-ship is not as grounded as we would like'. What happens in those conversa-tions when you are saying 'oh let's try this' or 'perhaps we can improve that'? I mean, I can't imagine what the conversation would be?

UK4: Well if it's very simple and straightforward, like ...' I would like to start our staff meetings with a silence', that's very much a 'fine if that's what you would like to do as the Head'. Then, that's fine because it's not, it's literally, you know, a minute or two and it's not imposing on anybody. It's kind of keep-ing that [the philosophical underpinning] way moving forward and we all felt and did it as a nice way to start a staff meeting.

In terms of how it is with, with girls, with the children, that might be on a staff meeting agenda. So we might talk about why use it? Why is the silence not so grounded? So one of the things we tried and one of the things we were talking about in ... with [particular school] Heads – all the Heads meet regularly – is that there's very often quite a lot of coughing and spluttering, whatever. So [here] in order to move towards a sort of a stronger silence, we decided as a staff that I would talk to the girls and say 'okay we're going to talk a little bit about our silence. How can we make that even better?' And I do that at the beginning of the year as well. I talk to them about [it], because obviously they've got all the new girls who arrive. And it's around saying 'so this is what you do with your time' as in, you know, there are lots of things you could do with that time [for silence in the meeting for worship]. 'These are the expectations that, that we have as a community of you'. And so at the beginning it's quite sort of shuffly. And then if we do, as a staff, say, 'actually this is not as good as we want it', it's about trying to articulate what it is about it that we think could be even better. So at the end, you know when we shook hands, earlier this year there was a great sort of performance of coughing and spluttering and shuffling. And [colleague] is acting deputy. So we've kind of slightly rearranged how we arrive in meeting. She now stays, and goes [only after everyone has left].

So it's about articulating what we're looking for, for the girls. So it's me saying 'look what we want to do is to allow you to take that silence, take that feeling with you into lessons for the rest of the day. If you have a huge great shuffle and a cough and a twitch, then you've negated the time you've just had'. So I think funnily enough making the silence in the [foundational underpinning context], making that as meaningful as possible for everybody, it's about being as articulate as you can about the silence, which is actually exactly what you are doing with your book isn't it? You are articulating something that within it has no articulation [laughs] at all. And so yes I suppose that's what we try and do here is to ... really ... dig away at what we're trying to achieve. Does that make sense?

HL: Yes, yes, absolutely.

UK3: ... um, because the other thing too is you can't just, it's not just one sort of set of practices which we are talking about with the silence practices – it's quite a number of other practices so, for example, we have the practice of everybody uses a fountain pen. Why? Because if you can get your attention to where the nib of the fountain pen is at the paper then you can hold it there which takes that silent presence and strength [and] your knowledge is going to fly out that fountain pen so to do that you've got to start to be attentive to the work. So each week we have a quality of work competition. We publish this book every year with the winners. It's trying to magnify the most beautiful work which is philosophically sound as well – Plato has a strong view about beauty but its impact comes on the level of attention and if you can be still and attentive, the work has never been better and if you can get still and attentive by doing, the work is going to get better, the sense of inner harmony is going to get better ...

UK4: ... silence is definitely something ...

HL: But that something. Can you describe it? What ...

UK4: I think it is ... something that ... enables thinking to happen in a way that it wouldn't necessarily happen if you were to do whatever you were doing in your mind. Okay, thinking, praying ... empty. I think collective silence enables a different thought process than the one, than a thought process you might have on your own. So I'm not saying that [specific type of practitioners of the type common to the school's underpinning philosophy] don't have silence on their own, I think they do. But in a school setting ... it, in my view, I, and all I know is what goes on in my head. It's different than when I'm on my own. And the combination, so we had the text this morning ... the combination of sort of the physicality [of] coming together, having something reflective to think about. Possibly somebody standing and sharing with them, with the group. I think it creates different thought processes.

HL: Of what kind?

UK4: I don't know. Because I, ... it may be, for me I do think about things ... think about the text or ... I, I don't, I don't know. But that's my thoughts. So that's my view on it. I think it encourages people to reflect maybe more deeply. Maybe gives them the courage of having other bodies around them, to think about things that might be a bit scary to think about on your own. You know, to really think about something in depth. So you have that. So 'right okay, today I am going to think about pursuing my dream or something difficult or whatever it happens to be because everybody is here and ...' Now there might be some ... I say to the girls when they are in Year Seven, 'you might want to think about your day ahead and sort your day out'. But even if it is ... everyday thinking, it will have a different kind of underpinning to it.

To me it's kind of like a visual thing of thinking, you know, it's kind of like a holding. It's like a ball, sort of holding, like a sort of underpinning, a strength, a soft strength. And you were talking about a strong silence.

HL: I mean after all it is ineffable [laughs] so it's hard to discuss isn't it?

UK4: Yeh, yes it is. But that's what I feel. That's what I, I get a sense that everybody goes away having felt held ... and that surely, if you feel held and you feel, you have strength from, from being held. You then have the strength to go into your school day and do your best thinking.

Cumulative practice makes strong silence

Part of the art of silence in schools is watching or noticing how time builds the silence in any given place and also how the silence preserves human energy. Silence as a practice occurs incrementally. There is no sudden overnight revelation and manifestation that silence has effects. The effects cumulate and become noticeable over time:

HL: I'm making a leap but I'm wondering if this sense of being held that you are talking about, is because life is hard work. And if there is this space where you are held briefly, does that mean that you can rest? Is that why there's this energy?

UK4: Possibly. That you can do that combination of rest and gathering energy. Is that what you mean?

HL: It is.

UK4: Yes.

HL: It just strikes me as almost strange. I mean things are strange, life is strange. But it strikes me as strange that such a short meeting, because it's only ten minutes isn't it, would be able to have effects like that.

UK4: I don't think just the ten minutes. I think it's cumulative. So you talk to Year Seven and they'll go 'oh yeh, that's okay. Yes we do that, quite like that. And now what's for tea?', sort of thing [HL laughs]. You know, and they'll be 'okay, yeah yeah yeah'. You talk to sixth form and they say 'I valued it more and more and I will take that with me into University and now I couldn't do without it'. And so I think it, I think it's cumulative.

Silence in action

The elements identified combine to create something in schools which use silence that is 'other'. The following part of the interview with UK2 captures the holistic nature of the educational elements of freedom, space, the art of silence in schools and the functions silence can have which profoundly affect what is educationally possible.

UK2: I've got to get your question clear. Why does the practice of silence allow an authoritarian set up to work well? Is that what you're asking?

HL: Well it's to do with resistance on the part of the children mostly. If you have an authoritarian set up where there isn't voice and something in the line of command is unfair for some reason and there's no way to say 'look I don't agree with that' and there's no space for it, is silence going to help those kinds of environments where unfairness is more likely because it's not well run or they don't have good resources or something? Can silence bring something to a set up that is struggling to function well?

UK2: I see. Erm, it would depend entirely upon how it was engaged in. I think you've got to have both. I think you've got to have a good structure, a healthy structure and ideally if you also had a bed of silence that the children would have recourse to you'd have a fantastic combination. I don't think that the implication or the assumption that the presence of an authoritarian structure or a disciplined structure is necessarily negative. I think it depends entirely upon how it's done.

HL: I suppose I am suggesting that there is a tendency for it to be able to be negative and I'm wondering if the addition of silence would lessen a possible tendency to ...

UK2: No I think the children just wouldn't take to it.

HL: To the silence?

UK2: Yes. Because you see what I've had to do here – and I say 'I' because it was presented to me to create a situation in which the young people desire to be quiet. You can't force that. You can't ever force a person to wish to meditate and, erm, that's a horrible mistake. It's worse than any other kind of external force, so you couldn't have it as part of your authoritarian structure. Now here it is true that all the girls will be required to sit together in silence. That I think is part of a structure like going to assembly or starting a lesson at this time and finishing at that time. That is good. That is healthy. That is conducive. So I've chosen to make that, if you like, compulsory that we will all sit together at this time and what the human being does in that time is entirely up to them. Entirely voluntary. The only rule that I ever put in is only that you should never interfere with another person's freedom to meditate, but there's no harm in just sitting quietly in consideration of others so that they can. But obviously one recognises that your deeper desire is to intro-duce them to the wonders of quietude so you have to grow a desire in them to want to go there as it were and that's the challenge.

HL: Do you do it slowly, do you do it quietly?

UK2: It's built up. It's built up. It's taken quite a number of years to create that environment. It needed turning round.

HL: I would imagine that you do that through trust, but is there something else?

UK2: Well, it is quite a few things and interestingly I think this is actually the core of all good education: create a desire in the young for that which is wonderful. You don't stuff it in but you make it available. You've actually got to germinate and inspire a desire to go for that. Well, you don't do it by force, you do it, as it were, by creating space, which is a subtle and emotional thing. Offering space. And once that space is offered, inspiring the desire to retreat.

Two things have helped a great deal, the person who's guiding it ... is very important. She or he has to have connected with that herself or himself, because the place from which she speaks will create that environment that will allow them to meditate. It will either switch them on or switch them off, essentially. And that is actually quite a subtle thing. It comes from deep within you and it resonates with the sounds and the words you choose to use. But two things have helped over time. One is the introduction of some music before mediating, which we've only done for the last 18 months or so, and that's really helpful. You have to choose the music incredibly carefully – which isn't easy – because not everybody hears what has to be heard when you set up music. But a couple of minutes of music is very evocative for quiet.

And the other thing that helps in a school a great deal is the example of older girls who love to meditate. So you didn't see this morning when you came in because on a Friday not everyone is there, but only half the school is there to meditate anyway because of the younger ones. But usually on the stage we have teachers and we have our sixth form prefects and once the girls start to want to meditate – the older girls – which grew over time, over the years, it became obvious to the younger ones looking at them that actually this is something they like to do. And occasionally girls will say I'd like to talk to the school about my experience of meditation. I've had that once or twice. It's very powerful. So it generates a culture that admires meditation or admires quietude and so now what I feel when we all sit together to meditate is a willingness to enter that opportunity. It wasn't like that for many years.

HL: Is it a skill you've got?

UK2: Um, well, yes and no. ... I suppose from the point of view of what I was saying about someone who guides it I'd say yes, I have those abilities, but it also has been a gradual generation of an environment. It's difficult to describe really. The school has grown over a number of years in a certain quality and I suppose it's just what you feed into it every year.

HL: So has that happened as a community?

UK2: Yes, as a whole community.

These excerpts suggest that silence is an artfully cared for function of the school's operation, which can create substantive and structural changes to the environment where education occurs.

Tangible outcomes of silence

Key to appreciation of silence as worthy of developing into a whole school ethos might be its potential educational outcomes in terms of exam grades. The headteachers I spoke to do not run schools where such foci are paramount. They are schools that consider good grades as desirable but not more important than general 'educational well-being'. Although some comments recognised additional benefits such as improved grades, overall the reports of academic benefits from silence in their schools were appreciative of the scholarly help silence brought, rather than instrumentally attuned to its uses:

UK3: Well, I think each boy has a timeline and you could draw an inverted bell curve and it goes like this [makes gesture] and it starts with a high level of enthusiasm for the silence practices – it's new and it's fresh – and they find some benefit, and they find some rest, and interestingly enough quite a lot of them talk about the release of stress! I mean, I can never remember talking at the age of eleven about stress, but they do. I say 'Why do you keep talking about stress?', and they say Mum and Dad are always talking about stress. So, age eleven or twelve there's quite a high level of enthusiasm. At the age of twelve, thirteen it begins to drop off a little bit, hormones begin to kick in a touch. At thirteen, fourteen, into the potentially horrible phase of human existence where everybody is a complete enemy, particularly Mum and Dad ... it begins to bottom off, fourteen, fifteen because now they are beginning to face public exams.

HL: How does that have an impact?

UK3: Because they recognise that stillness practices give them control over their minds, control over their attention.

HL: So it becomes useful?

UK3: So it becomes seen to be useful. And the boys that have continued with it even as that bell curve – and for them the bell curve is not quite so deep perhaps – through the age of eleven ... but almost everybody picks up ... and now they're hitting their GCSEs so they're back up to the top by the time they are sitting their GCSEs and my view – which is yet to be scientifically proven – my view is that we get the excellent academic results from a non-selective entry because of this practice.

HL: So it's seen to be useful. Who is seeing it as useful?

UK3: The boy. The boy sees it as useful ...

UK4: So here the culture is one that says 'Well, your thoughts are valid'. And you can, you know, you can share your thoughts. So the approach here is that just because you are a pupil doesn't mean you can think any less well than me as the teacher. So your thoughts are, you can think just as well as me. I might have the information to give you about the geography or the history or whatever. But actually as thinking partners, there is equality there.

HL: And do you think that comes from the fact that you use silence?

UK4: Yes I think what it means is when you go round or make sure that maybe you could slide into a class, it means that if there is silence in a classroom, because people are thinking, it's not a peculiar thing. So to have some silence to allow that thinking time is fine.

The focus in these schools on good outcomes through silence does not seem to be a means-end approach. Peim and Flint describe most schooling as replete with means-end usage of various tools that are not about the individual but about using the individuals for the sake of school improvement (Peim and Flint, 2012). Caranfa (following Picard) talks about how if 'shifting the mode of learning from discourse (knowing) to silence (unknowing), students come to value things not for the purpose of exploitation, profitability and utility, but for the spirit they contain ... in this relational mode, knowledge is not mechanised or depersonalised, and it is not seen as an end in itself' (Caranfa, 2004:227).

In the testimonies of these schools where silence is a feature of success, the success seems to be occurring at a deep human level that is entirely personal, and is thus shared by the community of the school. It is not impersonally instrumental:

UK1: [re pausing at the beginning and end of every lesson] Those moments of silence ... we call them ... that's what they're called but actually they are periods of being in touch with that life force ...

HL: What life force?

UK1: That thing! The thing I was talking about at the beginning. That common unifying essence of everybody. Talking about it sounds strange to me to hear myself ... it's very natural, very beautiful, very sincere, honest, and the children just love it. ... children are very naturally quiet and noisy ... it might go out of balance and go noisy and it's just a way of balancing. It's a kind of fresh start of it. Almost a fresh start and then a close of it ... English doesn't run into maths. It's very unifying because everybody is doing it.

HL: Does it make your life easier?

UK1: Yes it does! There's a start to something and an end to something and a time to reflect and it can provide inspiration for a lesson ... I don't know how teachers manage without it. It's just a way of gathering together everyone's attention ... it almost harnesses potential. It kind of brings it to a point you don't know where it's going to go to and that's exciting teaching ... and you sometimes find that the lesson takes off in a completely different way and that's very inspiring.

HL: Do you get resistance here [to the pausing]?

UK1: No. Very little.

HL: And have you noticed that in a community setting like this that there's an effect on communication that comes directly out of the fact that you're using silence – the irony of it, so to speak?

UK2: Well again I think that what silence does is it does open the gates to our deeper intelligence, our deeper sensitivity, so that when people communicate with each other they communicate more effectively. I think it enhances every-thing. Everything that you might call the best about our humanity.

You know the other thing is – I'm just thinking as you're asking these ques-tions – is that when you're meditating, when you're silent, your listening is very acute isn't it? Your hearing is very acute at a sensory level and deeper than would be available to you in ordinary, everyday life. You're attentive to what's going on and when you speak, you're aware of the sound of your voice, the effect of the sound of your voice, so I suppose what I'm saying is that the meditative practice heightens our awareness of the human apparatus and how to use it.

UK3: ... but do we wander around here with a great big flag up that says we're a school here that practices philosophy and practices stillness and speaks about these things all the time ...? No! We just get on with the business of everyday school life. People who come and spend some time here instantly comment on the spirit of happiness in the boys; relationship between the teachers and the boys; sense of composure that the boys have; sense of being unfazed by the stuff they are having to meet and to my mind, all of that comes back to their confidence in themselves because if a boy isn't confident in himself he won't easily fall still and silent and, paradoxically, if you can get him in some other way to fall still and silent then he will grow in confidence.

A change in attitude to silence in schools

Silence has established its educational credentials in schools such as these, towards perceiving silence as a valid part of the school environ-ment. Attitudes towards silence practices in schools are changing. The headteachers report such a change within their schools and also in the perceptions of others outside their schools that is fairly recent (see chapter five).

UK2: I mean, years ago – we've been meditating since the foundation of the school – but when I came in, which is fifteen, sixteen years ago ... the general attitude to meditation in society was that it was an iffy thing. Um, you know, cult and questionable, but now people respect it and almost every other interview that I have with 11 + candidates that are coming from all over the place, parents *and* the girls, are saying 'One of the things I really like about your school is the fact that you meditate and I'm looking forward to learning'. I mean that's really ... I find that amazing.

HL: The girls?

UK2: *Girls* themselves *in interview* and they're not just saying that to impress me.

HL: What sort of things do they say about ...

UK2: Well they say 'I'm really looking forward to meditating, I think it will do me a lot of good and I really would be helped by being still' and the parents are saying 'I know that stillness will enhance their development. She needs this and she's got all these characteristics but it will help her at regular intervals to withdraw and be still' – and these are parents who don't meditate.

UK3: ... so when a school like ours came along, which basically took the perspective that the place to begin an activity is in silence and stillness and the place to end an activity is in silence and stillness, we were initially regarded as somewhat strange and somewhat odd [by the group of boys' schools the UK3 school belongs to]. But now they've got to see it in operation, they have begun to change their view that it is even possible for a boy to be still.

UK2: ... I have heard of a number of people ... I heard of a school today – I can't remember which one it was but I've been doing a lot of 11 + interviews this term – and somebody said to me that they've started meditation with children in year seven or something – not with the rest of the school but they'd started practising meditation with year seven.

... I do think that the time is absolutely right for this because well, for two reasons. One, as you know there has been over the last five year there's been great concern about emotional wellbeing and we've got all sorts of things like the happiness agenda and wellbeing is now and has been a jargonised word, words, erm but I think people are waking up to the fact that silence is conducive to wellbeing.

Complexity

It is clear from what these headteachers said that silence in schools is far from straightforward. The benefits from meditation are not always immediately apparent or easy to gauge. In chapter five some of the research into the benefits of meditation practice is considered. What meditation is and where it starts, stops and where technique-less silence begins is also not clear-cut:

UK3: They [the boys] choose which method to use. They can change which method they want to use but if they've been introduced to transcendental meditation we recommend they stick to that. At least for a good long period so that they've tried it, because it doesn't necessarily show its immediate benefit or its immediate result.

UK2: My approach to silence is letting go, encouraging them to let go, and rightly or wrongly I don't manipulate that meditation. I don't know whether I've got the right touch on that or not but I tend to put in very little, in what I say or how I, I don't even really guide it particularly. As you know we offer a particular method of meditation which I think has a lot of value at different levels but it's really for them to discover. It's for them to discover either the value of that practice or quietness in general. Again it's rather creating the opportunity for them to discover the potential of it ...

HL: But the idea of meditation as a practice is possibly like education as a practice, whereas the idea of silence – isn't it something different?

UK2: It isn't a practice.

HL: From your point of view as an educationist do you think that introducing the concept of silence into schools is necessarily going to involve the concept of meditation?

UK2: No it doesn't have to. I think it would involve simply guiding the matter of letting go and being silent and it's really interesting – your question is interesting – because in a way meditation implies an action with a desire or an intent for an outcome and um if you like it's maybe the finest action left to the human being, the finest *doing* left to the human being that it should lead to a complete undoing, which is silence.

HL: Do you ... this question is to do with other schools. So here it's really organised around silence or the silence is well organised or well practiced and embedded and I'm wondering if you have any thoughts about educational spaces where that is not common or well understood in terms of ... Meditation is a big package, whereas you also use these pauses. Do you think for instance that pauses could be used in mainstream state schools?

UK2: Easily, and I think people are starting to do it.

UK1: Recourse to stillness and quiet is of fundamental importance in the school. Those moments provide anyone with freedom in a way. The people leading the school valued it and you can see the benefit it provides for the children. It's quite difficult to say how it benefits the children because we've never not done it.

UK4: ... you know, for me the most important thing ... it's not about getting into University. It's about giving, giving the girls choice and the belief they can do anything. Now if they want to leave school and have a family, the fact of the matter is that shouldn't be any less a choice than somebody who wants to be an astrophysicist. But the fact is they've had a choice that they want to do that. Not that that was the only thing open to them [laughs]. 'You know, actually this is what I want to do and it's a fully formed choice'. Or 'I want to go and fly to the moon'. And actually at a young age saying to them 'but you can do that. If you want to do that, you can do that'.

HL: But you think silence helps with this?

UK4: I think, I think it does yeh. I think it's around that core, that sort of inner core of real strength to ... yeh, for me it's the silence linking to the thinking, linking to the confidence without arrogance. To then going on and having aspirations for the future that are ... the other sort of thing is, around here it's about community. It's about silence with everybody. And it's around having aspirations that have grounding in wanting to contribute to the world and its future.

HL: But you are talking about a successful human life. I mean that's huge!

UK4: Yeh.

HL: Are you suggesting that ten minutes of silence and a little bit of a culture and cumulative practice allows that to happen?

UK4: I don't think it's the silence in isolation. It's around the community. Knowing what that's about, being able to articulate it. And part of ... if it's like a mind map, if we've got whatever we've got in the middle in a [particular type of] school or, or actually successful women as future, well I suppose it'd be a [particular type of] school here. What are the elements? And [silence] it's a key element. And you take that away and there'd be a gaping hole. And of course we can never know what the gaping hole would be. But ... it is an integral element. Yes I believe that very strongly ...

HL: It's funny that the children are so interested and keen on it isn't it!

UK4: If I were to take it ... ok, I would not be allowed to take it away! And that was one of the things [upon appointment] ... 'you're not going to take the silence away are you?' We can think about how we can make it even better. We might move timings, we might move ... but no, that stays. And the minute the girls ... the first people to come and see me here were the girls, making sure that that was gonna stay ... [then] they were fine. I could have done anything I wanted. Paint the grass pink! You know, do whatever. As long as that ... they were fine! [laughs].

A common philosophy and commitment

These schools suggested that the development of a whole school ethos of silence demands a serious commitment to working with silence in the long term, not as a gimmick or fashion. This ranges from sharing a common philosophy amongst staff and even students about silence as practice, to the recruitment of teachers:

UK3: Now in terms of the actual practice itself there are some days when it's absolutely wonderful. There are some days when it's as still as the depths of the ocean and there are other days when there is movement on the surface, clear movement on the surface and the important thing is not to worry about that. The important thing to know is that beneath the waves on the ocean there is the depth beneath the ocean which is always there. So in my view, um, the thing that enhances – gives real credibility and meaning to these stillness practices – is the philosophy behind it. These stillness practices would have an effect and be beneficial I'm sure without it but if you add the philosophy behind it you're adding, you're reaching the depth.

So the philosophy [here] is very simple. It's that every boy is a spiritual being. He is perfect, he is pure and he is free and he's eternal. In fact that's the contemplation we have and we reflect on: I am pure and perfect, free for ever. So the waves on the ocean are not disturbing the depth of the ocean. Even when he's moving. We've got a fellow called Jonny [pseudonym], he can't stop moving. He's an agitator – doesn't do it maliciously, he just agitates. He agitates himself and he agitates everyone around him, gets into and creates trouble, but it's not really him and if you keep reminding him that behind all that agitation is a pure, perfect and free being and keep looking at that and keep getting his attention turned back to that, then slowly, but slowly, he might be agitated today but by God! Twelve months ago he was off the wall ... I believe that these practices can get boys off their dependency on Ritalin for example. Every boy has an attention deficit problem. Every boy. It's just a question of degree and by seeing the real depth of the boy first and offering him these practices and not being worried or too concerned if he takes a little bit of time to get there, he will get there, he does get there.

HL: So this is an Atman [Hindu] philosophy [of the pure inner self] isn't it?

UK3: Hmmm [agreeing].

HL: ... so silence practices in a school where they introduce pause and meditation options and so on without the Atman philosophy, do you think that it would last?

UK3: I think it would be difficult because I think that people could be blown off course, just by the breezes of life ... you might abandon these things and say 'well, ahh it's not working' ...'

HL: And ... the silence, out there, is considered a bit strange. So it's a culture thing isn't it? Do you have thoughts about how a culture like that gets created? Clearly it's been created here in a particular way or for particular reasons.

UK4: How is that created? Well I suppose for [this kind of] school, it was there right at the very beginning. So I don't know how easy or not it would be to take that into another setting and you are talking a little bit about how that can be useful ... in other schools in the maintained sector. I think you'd have to think very carefully about it. And it would take a long time. I think we, we talk a lot about ... we talk lots about what we do as a [particular] school. We talk about our meetings. We talk about how can we encourage an even better, if you like, silence, a stronger silence. I like that, yeh. How can we get them to go stronger and stronger and stronger. And ... I think it's about creating an awareness and creating sort of conversations around what you are trying to do and explain, you know, articulate the value.

So for me and now perhaps if I were to think about 'How could I inculcate this in another setting?', it would be around ... talking about looking at what that school has. Where that is at the moment and seeing if there are any gaps, or any things that could be helped by perhaps introducing a bit of silence or whatever. And kind of creating conversations around it. I think it would take, I think it takes a long time. I mean there are lots of things here so we don't have ... we don't have bells in between lessons. That might be something you could transfer to another school immediately. Say 'okay let's try and have less bells' so that it's not just being silent. It's about sound and ... how that might work ... So I know that there are lots of things that you couldn't transport to another setting. Because as [the deputy headteacher] was saying, it's about having an understanding of what is underpinning the silence.

Whereas at [another school], it's a different underpinning. And I don't know, well it would be interesting wouldn't it. It would be interesting to say 'oh look, let's have some thinking time in another school' and see what that felt like. Certainly with the junior school – because we have a junior school from age three to eleven – I try and get them to do their very best thinking in silence for fifteen seconds. And see how, and then they do that and they do that very well. So it's just by stages I think, if you were to think about bringing [it] into another setting ...

The role of staff in a whole school silence ethos

The headteacher appears especially important in shaping a philosophy to underpin the silence practice and foster commitment to the art of silence in schools. That the Head has some personal practice of silence and an understanding of how it functions and what it can do seems to be necessary for a whole school ethos for silence to take hold:

HL: Does running a school with those kinds of philosophies and practices involved require a particular kind of headteacher?

UK3: Yeh, I think so, I think so. So I think to run a school like this you would have to have some holistic vision for the boy ...

HL: What is specific about this school that's to do with silence?

UK3: Silence is the critical unifying factor. So I probably inadequately expressed it. There are two dimensions to the work on silence. One is to do with spiritual emotional growth of the child. In the silence, the child should see that the differences which divide and aggravate and cause much distress in the world – the differences of gender, the differences of sexuality, the differences of religion – these are very surface things, these are waves on the surface, these are not real.

The reality of the person you are dealing with is a sense of being which is silent and through your silence you can meet that sense of oneness and unity. So that's one dimension. The second dimension is the impact of silence on the educational processes. And you see that by the strengthening of the powers of attention. And with the stronger powers of attention which emerge from the silence the academic results which you get in the end of the exercise will be far stronger. What I would look for in the school, and do look for in the school, is a sense of openness. A sense of oneness. A sense of great tolerance and a sense of great compassion ...

HL: And that relationship with the teacher and the student you mentioned, how is that different from another school's?

UK3: Well there's a lot of good relationships in a lot of other schools, so by what I say I don't judge other schools but, um, you do get a sense that because the teacher is encouraged by the Head to look to that pure perfect and free being underneath the waves, um, that the teacher is responsive to the needs of the child each day. So the boy who came into your classroom this morning is not the boy who came in this afternoon. He is in his essence, but the waves can change. How do you deal with the waves changing? By knowing his essence is the same. So your stillness comes back to the starting point of it and from that you deal with it and come back to everything. That's the idea ...

HL: Could I ask – to do with [another school which uses mindfulness practices] I wonder: philosophy plus silence ... mindfulness but there is no philosophy [in the school as a whole connected to the mindfulness philosophically] so I wonder what you think about what they're doing?

UK3: It's got clear scientific evidence supporting its usefulness in therapeutic environments and therefore I think you would logically assume that it must have some value in an educational setting. It must have some value. So we were very pleased to hear that that sort of initiative was taking place. I feel that as far as a headmaster or a headmistress is concerned, you have to have some underpinning of that to keep it going, day in, day out, day in, day out. Through the rough, through the smooth, through the good, through the bad and not be deflected from the fact that there are so many agitations and waves possible in a school day, that you might be thinking that this isn't of value to them. You've also got to have some underpinning so that the staff remain with you. So, for example every day we begin here with the staff 'office'. Every day we spend two or three minutes silently together in the staff room. We have a reading ...

HL: So you've come into it and ... perhaps you've come upon silence. You've discovered it by coming here?

UK4: I don't know because part of my interview was ... quite an in-depth, an intense discussion around my spirituality. I'm from a [religious] background so I'm used, it's not alien to me. But I've had to learn quite a lot about the whole thing. But I, the learning is fine as long as you feel comfortable. I see the value in it. It's no good coming here saying 'oh well we're not gonna do that or ...'. You know, it's around seeing what have we got and how is it possible to move with the times. And all schools [of this kind] do things slightly differently. But there is that silence.

In addition to the headteachers being interested personally in silence, teaching staff need to respect silence in the school. Their attitude is said to be crucial in supporting the relationship to silence as an abiding ethos that a school might wish to develop:

> **UK3**: But I think a lot of people are attracted by the sense of presence now ... living in that moment now, learning mind control, learning to control your mind, learning to be focused and attentive and lots of teachers are inspired by that, so we go fishing for teachers from that pond ... our advertisements are very clear, to appeal to people in that pond ...

> **UK3**: We've also done it from day one. The way we apply it has changed. We've found a new educational approach to parents looking for an experience. We've found a better language to discuss things with them.

> **HL**: Translation of your approach into mainstream schools is very hard ...

> **UK3**: Very

> **HL**: So you have thoughts on translation?

> **UK3**: Well I agree it's very hard, because first and foremost you need to get the staff with you ...

Silence as a promoter of happiness

The schools which had a commitment to silence were happy places. This was an outstanding feature of the testimonies and self-assessments and I felt it myself when I entered the schools.

> **HL**: So is there a sense of purification that comes through the practicing of silence or does it happen in another way?

> **UK2**: I wouldn't call it purification. I think it's just really probably just as I said. It just allows the process to, it's like water – it just nourishes it because the root, erm – again these words are very difficult – but if you take that spirit of love at its very root, erm, is in our human understanding silence, so every time a person sort of enters that being, enters that silence, they enter that ocean of love.

> **HL**: So how does that affect the way the school functions?

> **UK2**: It doesn't affect the way the school functions but I think somehow what it seems to generate here and I can only say this because people say it to me, is two things: one is that the girls are happy and the other is that there is a great spirit of love and it just happens.

Conclusion

What these interview excerpts tell us is that silence is considered by those in schools with silent features as a significant element of the school and the education it provides. It acts as an integral and unifying element. It is conducive to personal and school success.

This unity and success comes at a price. Schools thinking about adopting silence as a part of practice need to consider certain matters. What these headteachers tell us can be summarised as follows:

■ A relationship to silence forms that is as demanding as a personal relationship. Silence needs attentive respect if it is to 'talk' in a school setting. Its presence is the result of artful work of listening to it in action. What that actually means is the result of experience and no doubt trial and error. Whatever the content and nature of the journey, silence as a feature of a school and as a presence that can be encountered is generous in response to attention and can easily be accessed by all, when the effort is made.

■ Silence in schools as a feature needs to be attended to cumulatively and its benefits brought out incrementally.

■ Silence offers psychological space. This space is good for reflection towards new learning and educative development. It enhances the capacity for curiosity, freedom of choice, wonder, new and perhaps unusual lines of thinking.

■ From practices of various kinds, silence generates enhanced levels of well-being that can translate into interpersonal harmony and raised self-esteem.

■ Techniques of silence are either substantial in that they require some form of initiatory training such as with meditation or mindfulness practices, or they are technique-less because they do not require training. Deliberately and by electing to do so, waiting, pausing, staring, pondering, sitting and just being aurally silent whatever the action can all be examples of technique-less silence.

■ Silence creates atmospheres that have less friction than might otherwise be the case because people work inter-personally with a calmer mindset and more reflection. People may also be more neurologically at ease, suggesting that resistances and upsets are slower to form. The atmosphere can be easy-going and pleasant because silence is an aspect of the school's ethos.

- Schools with silence as a whole school feature are considered to be different from schools without such an atmosphere because interpersonal contacts function with a mysterious smoothness.

- Silence in schools allows a focus on good academic results but allows this to be done non-instrumentally and without the learning and teaching being directed by a means-end mentality. Good results emerge, rather than being forced.

- Silence in schools is entering the mainstream as a part of educational practice.

- Silence in schools is demanding and requires patience.

- A philosophy of some kind might be needed to underpin silence practice. This could be a religious philosophy or it could be a belief in the potential for silence to bring democracy into a school. The whole school needs to share a belief in the value of silence for it to become a whole school ethos.

- Silence as a whole school ethos is in theory accessible to all but in practice it depends on certain circumstances and commitments in a school being in place.

An empirical evidence base for the value of techniqued silence practices with children, such as mindfulness and meditation, is only beginning (Burke, 2010). The long term experience of the practitioners who speak here has much to add to our growing understanding of what silence in schools might offer. Their accounts point not only to techniqued practices of silence, but also technique-less practices that have developed over the years in these schools. The awareness of the art of silence shared by these practitioners is an extremely important contribution to the growing 'science' of silence in schools. Faith – a secular belief that is happy enough to trust in irrationality – is required. Most interestingly, perhaps, for those who demand scientific evidence to underpin silence practice with children, is the spiritually inclined nature of some of these comments. How science and spirituality can meet in the arena of silence is an interesting matter for research, which some are looking at through the lens of well-being (eg. Campion, 2009).

It is clear that practitioners in successful silence schools have for years been combining all the elements that research needs to investigate. The attitude of these practitioners to silence, as a fulsome part of the school, is possibly why silence is so successful for them. Their integral use of meditative practices sits within this ethos and benefits from it:

> Meditation has the potential to be an effective form of school-based health promotion, given the associated broad spectrum of benefits. A whole-school approach appears to facilitate better implementation. (Campion, 2011:35-36)

It appears that a whole-school approach to silence is optimal. Some kind of underpinning attitude or philosophy for this approach appears necessary to sustain such an environment.

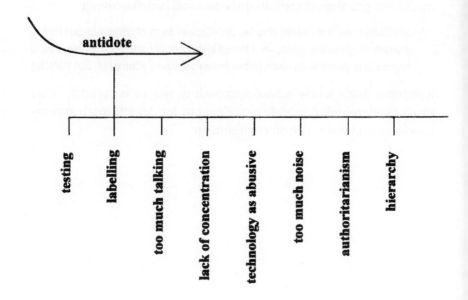

testing

labelling

too much talking

lack of concentration

technology as abusive

too much noise

authoritarianism

hierarchy

antidote

3
Silence practices in schools with no ethos of whole school silence

Introduction

S chools are perceiving the value of silence in ways that challenge prevailing ideas of educational 'value'. As Max Picard says, silence has a character that contradicts and counteracts schooling for improvement and instrumental means-end change:

> Silence is the only phenomenon today that is 'useless'. It does not fit into the world of profit and utility; it simply is. It seems to have no other purpose; it cannot be exploited ... you cannot get anything out of it. It is 'unproductive'. Therefore it is regarded as valueless ... It interferes with the regular flow of the purposeful ... It gives things something of its own holy uselessness, for that is what silence is: holy uselessness. (Picard, 2002:18-19)

The 'interference' that silence offers becomes useful for schools. Its ability to be outside the various demands and pressures of improvement (Peim and Flint, 2012), becomes an antidote to a world of mainstream education that has lost its way in a forest of measurements, assessments and demands for evidence and standards (Delandshere, 2001).

Criticism of a 'what works' mentality is widespread in the educational research literature. Evidence-based practice attitudes calling for effectiveness fail to ask 'effective for what?' (Biesta, 2007). It is argued that any loss of focus on the intrinsic *purpose* of an education for children goes against good educational practice:

... a case can even be made that sometimes educational strategies that are not effective, for example because they provide opportunities for students to explore their own ways of thinking, doing and being, can be more desirable than those that effectively proceed towards a pre-specified end. (Biesta, 2009:36)

Problems arise when education is not approached holistically as a multi-level and multi-natured event, but when, instead, something concrete is put centre stage that is considered effective, has been measured and here is the league table to prove it. Delandshere argues that schooling systems are now using an historically inherited formation of concepts regarding assessment without questioning the nature of their genesis. She quotes Wilbrink:

It is fascinating to observe that assessment procedures handed down by tradition were in this century uncritically adopted in mass education, possibly leading to major inefficiencies in education and, for too many students, a lack of quality in school life. (Wilbrink, 1997, in Delandshere 2001:119)

Delandshere maintains that an assessment culture (towards 'improvement') in schools is limiting, unreal and distorting. It fails to capture the nature of knowledge as a sociological, ethical and political construction:

The system of beliefs, values and purposes in which the agents involved are participating is rarely discussed. The perspectives taken when stating evaluative judgements are often assumed to be understood and agreed upon, when in fact they are rarely explicit or public, and hence, not open for scrutiny or discussion. (Delandshere, 2001:121)

In such a system silence is opening school experience up to a freedom from measurements. A mentality which requires evidence, assessment and justification closes off many possibilities, whereas silence opens and allows exploration possibilities. The desire is for education to be a transaction rather than a determination. This would afford it democratic status (see Biesta, 2007) and prevent abuses of power (see Harber, 2004). It allows the possibility for freedom of personal and intimate kinds (Stronach and Piper, 2008) and the idea of community voice (Fielding, 2010).

In schools subject to pressures of league tables and which have a mentality of assessment and measurement, can silence offer escape? In the previous chapter we saw that silence is used by some schools to offer space for reflection and to just be; to think original thoughts and to find the self-confidence to pursue inner realisations and expression. Silence also offers a more transactional form of education, touching in spirit the integral forms of substantial democracy that many educationists see as essential for schooling. This aspect of the democratic is discussed in chapter six.

Isolated silence practices in schools

In some schools there are teachers who recognise that silence is something of value although there is no underpinning philosophy to sustain silence practices and no whole school ethos of silence. Yet silence practiced in pockets is still of benefit. Silence in such circumstances enters into schools through a teacher who has personal experience of some form of silence they believe could benefit the class and the school. The teacher in the UK5 interview is one example, illustrating how silence is introduced and what effects it seems to have. UK6 is a teacher who stumbled upon silence as a powerful aspect of their classroom when Silent Fridays – days of quiet reading – were introduced on a regular basis.

Silence worked into school experience, by some teachers for some students, functions differently from silence as a whole school approach. It is isolated and possibly open to forms of taint and reduced effects because there is no shared ethos across the school community. Yet it seems to survive robustly. The key role of a headteacher as support for silence in schools is becoming recognised (eg. McMahon and Mahony, 2011). Isolated silence practice is becoming a significant school-based intervention. There are questions to be asked concerning the appropriateness of teachers taking it upon themselves to develop silence as change. Alternatively, these practices could be seen as part of the professional free will of a teacher, introduced without senior management consultation as part of a teacher's style and freedom of choice in classroom management. It would depend on factors such as the nature of the silence and even what it was called. 'Mindfulness' or 'meditation' sessions, for instance, would require parental agreement, given that they may sound religious and this then would involve the headteacher. On the other hand a teacher might read about silence and simply begin and end their lesson with a minute of silence. Is that a matter for a head-teacher? Perhaps not. A teacher might choose to offer to students an opportunity to work quietly on a regular basis. Is this a matter for a head-teacher? Why would it be? Yet silence in any form – where it is part of choice and choosing – stands to be a strong force in a school that would have effects outside specific classrooms. Isolated silence in a school setting comes with questions, intrigue and outcomes – even isolated silence practice is a community issue: a whole school approach.

Embracing silence on the curriculum

In schools which do not advertise an ethos of silence for the children – that a family joining that school already has understood and embraced – the practice of isolated silence must be part of *choice*. Silence will not be strong if it is not presented as a new curriculum feature that can be taken or not. Without a whole school ethos which accepts silence practices, silence on a school curriculum needs careful negotiation. This is not easy in schools where most curriculum features are imposed without child-centred collaboration or consultation.

I asked a practitioner of mindfulness silence practices (see chapter five) in a school that otherwise shows no interest in these practices, what they thought of the idea that children are being enmeshed in silence experiences at the whim of a teacher. The testimony indicates a number of substantial differences in approach to silence from those in schools with an agreed whole school ethos described in the previous chapter. The differences are mostly caused by incommensurabilities between how silence works and can be introduced to children who are and are not familiar with it in a school. But there are also commonalities: chiefly that silence takes work and commitment, wherever and however it is found functioning in a school setting. Importantly, the following interview excerpt shows how central to isolated silence practices is the idea that it is voluntarily taken on by the children to whom it is introduced.

UK5: For us the crucial thing is the whole course has been written for conscript audiences. What that means is if you really want mindfulness to take off, you've got to, to some extent, persuade and I'd even use the word 'sell', the concept of mindfulness to young people. You know, they've got to, particularly with adolescents, understand why they are doing it and what's in it for them kind of thing ... adolescents have been programmed to develop their own identity and kick against things and challenge. And so what you are partly doing is you are persuading them that mindfulness is a good thing. You know, that it's worthwhile. And you are sowing the seeds there. Now I think the great thing is, is if you can get that right, if you can persuade a conscript classroom that mindfulness is beneficial and they can experience those benefits directly, then it opens the door to any context. Then, if you have a voluntary group so much the better. If you have children who want to learn about mindfulness, so much the better ...

HL: A school is a powerful machine and I can imagine that if you as a teacher, or anybody, went to the boss, headteacher, and said 'this is really good, here's all the research, I'm an expert in it, would you like something like that in the school, given its benefits, and so on' and so the boss would say 'oh, sounds like a good idea'. Exam results go up or whatever catches their imagination. So then the machinery of the school would put that in place for the children because there's a sense that schools do good things for kids. I'm wondering what in that process, where, where does the child who doesn't want to do it go? I mean because there is this sense in education, we introduce children to things that they really don't know are good for them but that are good for them. And that's part of education.

UK5: Well that's where it comes down to enjoyment. I don't think any kid minds doing something they enjoy. And that's what [our course] is written to do. It's to get them to enjoy it. You know, part of it is ... we give ... how familiar are you with sort of MBCT, MBSR courses? Have you been on one or do you know what they are like?

HL: I'm a meditator but I've never been on one of these courses ...

UK5: They're good, it's worth trying. The first meditation that you do on adult mindfulness courses, you do lying down. Well, the first practice you do is a raisin exercise. But then once you've done that and you've discussed that and you've drawn some learning from that, you do a ... and various other sort of group bonding type activities ... you do a body scan. A lying down body scan. Now if you try doing that with a class of kids, it could be total chaos! ... You've got a tight classroom with thirty kids in. You've got to get them all lying on the floor. You could imagine that could be carnage! But actually we don't really mind that too much. I mean I think with practice you can get it right. And you can actually get them very quiet. And you can do it with a whole class. But it might not work. But we wouldn't really regard that as failure as long as they're coming out with positive associations about mindfulness. Then there's the sense that you have at least jumped over one hurdle which is they associate mindfulness with what is interesting, engaging, beneficial hopefully, but certainly not negative ... It's not like trying to teach them Latin, which I would love all children to learn. But you can imagine people kicking against that: 'what's the point, oh it's really boring!' and all the normal things that kids would say about Latin.

HL: Well there's, you, you fully appreciate these things and I can imagine the kids having a really sympathetic attitude to you. I mean yeh, in a scenario where the teacher was not as experienced/sympathetic as you. What if a kid, I mean in your experience, what if a kid kind of actually disliked the teacher and was refusing to do anything for that teacher?

UK5: Well I mean that's why – it's a very good question – that's why we want to take it into different schools because we haven't really come across that yet. But in a way it would be good to do that. I would say that you would only get that situation if you get teachers teaching it who either don't understand it or don't practice it.

Teachers as practitioners

It is suggested that there is a need for teacher practitioners in schools to be an embodiment of the kinds of calm and peace which silence practices can help to instil: 'just as swimming teachers need to be able to swim ...' (Burke, 2010:134). UK5, who is a practitioner of mindfulness, considers that not only do teachers seeking to introduce silence into schools need to be practitioners of silence practices themselves, but they also need to be personal role models for silence. There is a suggestion, not without grounds, that silence in a person's life would make them calmer and therefore a better embodied role model for others taking up the effort of practicing silence.

UK5: I think the worst thing you can get is a teacher teaching mindfulness who doesn't do it. Or a teacher teaching mindfulness who doesn't embody it. If you're a kid, if you've just come out of a class where you've been taught by teacher A as being reduction for stress and anxiety and anger and all of these things. And then you all gather in the classroom and after lunch you see the same teacher having a blazing row with a colleague and shouting – you are gonna think 'well hang on, what's this about?' Whereas if the teacher practices, understands, feels the benefits of mindfulness, then the children pick that up. It's that classic thing in schools between what is taught and what is caught.

That is, as important as the [content] knowledge that they get from their geography, maths, English, history, science teachers, is what they learn from the way the teacher holds [her/]himself. How does he walk into the class-room? How does he ask them to be quiet if we're dealing with silence? You know, how does he behave when he's under pressure. What's he like when he's tired. Or what's she like when she's upset with a pupil or when some-body's disappointed that pupil. You know, all of these things, how they behave, how a teacher behaves and is in the class, is, is of crucial impor-tance. And that's probably connected with your idea of strong silence. I think in a way it's all in that arena of teacher conduct and embodiment and this idea of what's caught and what's taught. In a school where there is strong silence, they would catch that and appreciate it. And culturally you can really see that it would embed.

This idea of silence becoming embedded through modelling amongst staff is seen in examples of schools where 'positive values' are promoted (Farrer, 2000).

Silence for children with problems and/or in difficult schools

This interview respondent was interested in exploring what effect mindfulness practice could have in school settings which were far from calm and where children might bring troublesome issues to school. This teacher believes that experiencing silence could be a revelation:

UK5: ... when I've spoken to kids actually in more difficult schools about mindfulness and what they've learnt, there's almost a sense of ... you know, I don't like the word because it has religious connotations but almost sort of an epiphany kind of realisation. Sort of moments of 'oh my goodness, I didn't realise that I could be, that I could feel like this through a simple practice like paying attention to my breath ...' So I actually think because the wellbeing level with troubled youngsters is so intense it might be that this dose that you give them [of mindfulness practice] could have a much higher effect. But this is total speculation ... I think the potential for epiphany could be greater in more difficult schools. That would be my hypothesis. The reason being that in a very stable secure safe environment – one might argue a slightly more privileged environment – there's only so much improvement that can hap-pen. Whereas I think in a more difficult environment with kids that just are not familiar, they haven't experienced, they come from circumstances which challenge their minds and everything, every day at a fundamental level. The lack of stability in a home is something which most of the kids here don't have to deal with. Whereas if at home you have ... if there's no stability at home, then imagine the mind that they bring into schools. And then imagine if a teacher who knows that group and who is skilled enough to work with that

45

group introduces them to the calm, the quiet, the potential stillness of mind-fulness – then that's a huge transformation that could be witnessed there.

Research conducted in pupil referral units and prisons, using meditative techniques with people manifesting troubled mental states, has found that the use of silence practices fairly quickly allowed their minds to reach a state of improved wellbeing and interpersonal behaviour (eg. Abrams and Siegel, 1978; Dye, 2001). Research amongst a 'non-troubled' group showed the most benefit to be for adolescent boys 'higher in anxiety or neuroticism (low emotional stability), and who arguably are most in need of an intervention' (Huppert and Johnson, 2010:271). Despite their suggestion that a differential effect might be found in people of different socio-economic backgrounds experiencing differing life circumstances, the practitioner interviewed saw mindfulness as a leveller and as belonging to inherent human equality. This aspect is developed further in chapter six.

UK5: ... for instance, let me give you a very simple practice that we did. A first practice that we did with the children is in the introduction, and we introduced the concept of the mind. And the first slides challenge the kids about what is the mind, where is your mind? It's more simple than this, but if I have to sum it up that's effectively what we're asking them. And you ask them where their mind is and they point to their heads ... And then you say 'okay so that's where your mind is', right. And you say 'hold out your hand as if you're holding a basketball', yeh. And they hold out their hands, sort of, I don't know, about a foot apart. And they just hold them there. And you say 'okay so now I'd like you to place your attention in your hands. Just closing your eyes if you need to and feeling your hands. Not looking at them at all. Look at me or look wherever. And just pay attention to what you can feel in your hands, or direct your attention there'. And then I leave them for a bit and you can see what's happening ... They are sitting there and they are absolutely spellbound. Not by you but by these sensations that they get in their hands. You know, fizzing, tingling, buzzing. And then you say to them 'okay, so now where's your mind?' And they go 'in my hands'. They often go 'whoooaa', you know, 'that was a bit strange' ... And I think that's a bit of an epiphany. It's the simple realisation that attention can be directed and that in the direction of attention comes a certain intensity of experience.

Some of them actually shake their hands. I mean it can even creep out some of them a little bit if you are not careful. Because they just have never felt that before. You do get some who can't feel anything at all sometimes. In which case you can turn that into a group activity and you ask them to clap their hands really hard, then pay attention. And they can usually feel the warmth there. Now I think that's completely independent of any social economic demographic. I think it's just a function of the human mind that you're introducing people to ... It's a characteristic of our mind ... that is available to anybody. And I think that's why mindfulness as a training is such a powerful one ... I think it works independently of a lot of these, these [socio-economic] factors ...

Building an ecology of silence in a school with only isolated practice

The headteachers in chapter two talked about silence as an ethos which is underpinned in the school by its history and philosophy. The teacher below is working amongst some colleagues who are sympathetic to the idea of mindfulness but it is outside the school ethos. He appreciates the idea of what he called an 'ecology' of silence in a school but believes that an awareness of silence as 'ecological' takes time to embed and needs to be artfully applied.

UK5: ... I had a very lovely present actually from an art teacher here, of a little white bowl. He was a potter, and the bowl was one that he'd crafted. And he said it was inspired by something I'd said to him about the sort of effect, if you like, of mindfulness once you've started practicing, which is that until you've experienced a mind which is quiet, you have no idea that that mind is possible. But once you do touch that space, and I'm not talking about any profoundly deep state of, you know of 'jhana' concentration. But once you have attained ... no, no! attained makes it sound like you've got there. Once you just experience directed attention, even for a few seconds, it gives a reference point. And the brain doesn't forget that reference point. And so when it's noisier, it now has something to compare that brain noise to. It has a moment of quiet.

And the way I normally describe that is using my hands and with my right hand I kind of whirl my hand around and say 'that's what the brain feels like normally'. And as long as that's all that's happening, that's all the brain knows. And then I hold up my left hand and hold it completely still and clench the fists slightly and describe that as a still point. Then suddenly my right hand which is doing all this noise and moving around and activity, is aware that there is this other bit of it which can be, this other hand, which is still. It has a reference point. And that, that quiet can become a reference point.

HL: Putting that into a wider school context. I mean there are two questions. One is, right so this hand, the two hands are a metaphor for a school okay, in this question. ... I'd like to know what you think about that in terms of your experience of [your school] and also a more sort of, a wider consideration of that as a metaphor for a school environment?

UK5: I think that's a brilliant metaphor. ... I think it's a very, it has to be a very gradual thing. I mean what has to happen is ... I think one of the most important things is that the teachers embody ... the kind of values that come with mindfulness. Patience, tolerance, kindness, understanding, allowing, accepting. All of the words that you'll pick up in any [Jon] Kabat-Zinn book. Now those are things which teachers really have to embody before pupils can. And I think depending on the school, how you introduce teachers to these things is a very important and delicate process which you can't force. I mean I've been doing this here for four or five years now. And I think what's lovely is that there's a greater understanding of what it is I'm bringing into the school. If not, if not a sort of ... if not participation by everyone, there is at least an understanding and hopefully a sort of healthy respect for what it can bring with it.

What I don't think you can do is ever force anybody to practice effectively. I don't believe you will get schools where every teacher will sit quietly for a certain period of time every day. I mean, if you could, absolutely wonderful! And in a small school, perhaps even a small primary school you might be able to do that. But I think in a secondary school you've got teachers who have their own passions. They have their own drives, they have their own subject loves. Everybody has what makes them tick. And to suddenly expect everybody to think that mindfulness is what makes them tick, I don't know that's realistic. And that even, perhaps even worries me slightly as that could be sort of slightly faddish. You know, everybody gets into it suddenly and then it goes. That's what I would want to resist.

I think for me mindfulness should be a part of the school ecology. Just like English teaching is or music is or drama is or sport is. ... I think a healthy school has to have that kind of ecology of interested individuals. And I think it would be unrealistic perhaps to expect all of those individuals to suddenly become passionate about mindfulness. ... what I think you could expect and cultivate with perhaps mindfulness in it, would be this idea of strong silence. You know, strong silence I think, because it's not a practice, it's more of a culture. Which mindfulness practitioners would contribute specifically to but which everybody could get in the sort of non-threatening way ... it doesn't oblige you to necessarily meditate every day at all. I just think this idea of a silence being a strong silence rather than a weak silence, you can see that being cultivated through school assemblies being managed in the right way. School teachers managing their classrooms in the right way. I think the idea of a strong silence fits into an ethos which is ... which I imagine could be embedded.

HL: How?

UK5: I think through a headteacher probably who believes in it ... actually can I backtrack slightly? ... we've been talking a lot about calm and quiet and stillness of the mind. Mindfulness is not just about that. That is an aspect of it. But mindfulness is also about dealing with the mind when it's choppy and observing the mind when it's difficult, which might even make it worse for a period of time. And [once] learnt, placing mindfulness in the context of stress, anxiety, anger is critical. But how would you do it? Okay, I think what you would do is, well I hope we're going to do here next year, is we will be ... all of year ten will learn mindfulness via the nine week course. Now that means that ... by the time those boys get to year thirteen which is the top year, you'll have four years of the school who understand mindfulness. And hopefully there would be a, some sort of top-up lesson. I'm very anti-evangelical and anti-forcing people. So I think once you've done the nine week course I don't think you should get too heavy with them about it. But I think you should, you know, sew it through.

So, for instance, in year eleven when they have GCSEs, before their GCSEs you might have a session with all of the year elevens and do another exercise and remind them and refresh them about what this course is, what it taught them the previous year. So, by the time they get to year thirteen, all four years know about mindfulness. And I think that means that if you had an assembly service where ... periods of silence were built in, in a sort of Quakeresque kind of way where silence became normal and accepted and appreciated, then it might be that schools begin to change. And I think that is probably possible. But it requires a very interesting mix of character to deliver that. And it might be ... is it possible? I don't know – but I'd be interested to hear what you think but I know that's not what ...

HL: ... well, this is going to be in the book actually because I have spoken to schools that have, and where it is possible. And it's happening. And the things that they identify, the ways that can be possible are that it is long term. That it's been going on for a while ... and that it's built up through the years.

UK5: Definitely.

HL: ... I mean the thing that I'd be interested to hear from you ... In these schools where it's working they have a strong philosophy ... What sort of philosophy would a secular school have that would be ... they suggest that a philosophy is required to underpin consistent and ...

UK5: Yeh, yeh interesting. It's a very interesting question. I suppose mindfulness could be a philosophy that underpins a secular school. It would be partly the practice of mindfulness but it would be more the values that go with mindfulness practice. As I said, things like patience, kindness, tolerance, equanimity, allowing, accepting. Those sorts of words which would really benefit the school in terms of its anti bullying processes and in terms of the concentration in exams. And, you know there's loads of potential benefits of having ... those values underpinning a school. I mean I don't think they're religious values necessarily. I mean I think they are but they could be secularised. Well they could be presented in a secular context. I don't think there's anything wrong there. Compassion is another one ... compassion is sort of the unwritten part of the mindfulness course which is so much easier to teach when you teach mindfulness in a spiritual context and so much harder to convey in a secular context without it seeming like some form of prayer. I think that's the next plank in mindfulness training. It's certainly the next challenge, I think, for [our course] to find a way of explaining the importance of kindness and compassion without it feeling like there's some sort of spiritual agenda behind that.

HL: You know, you've identified that there's a, well I picked up a sense from what you've said and tell me if I'm wrong, that one person believing in this stuff and knowing how to do it, maybe even also practicing it and showing practice to others in a school is not enough for an ecology.

UK5: I think that's correct because I think if I left the school at the moment, then mindfulness would go with me and that's not to say that there's opposition at all. In fact it's been very touching, the level of support that I've had from the headmaster and senior management team and the kids. There's no anti-mindfulness thing. There was a ripple at the beginning, a concern amongst the Christian community that this might be some form of Buddhism by the back door. But all it took was for me to just literally show the curriculum to those concerned and say 'look this is secular training' and they really accepted that because, you know, it *is* secular training. There is no agenda there. However, you need more ... teachers to do it. I mean it's interesting – do you need an explicit endorsement rather than an implicit one? I don't know the answer to that.

HL: Where would that come from if it was implicit?

UK5: It would have to come from the Head, I think. Unless the Head is lead-ing it ... I think you are never really going to succeed ... to begin with at least. I think what could happen is one Head could lead it and if he establishes it well enough then the next Head would just pick it up when they arrived. Be-cause they'd feel it's a, it's a vibe and a culture that they wouldn't want to lose because it would be quite precious in a way – quite a delicate and important part of the ecology. But I think to begin with you'd really have to have a head-teacher to, to sew it through ...

In chapter five there is discussion of the growth of silence practices in schools and how it is spreading. This teacher is aware of his practice as part of a situation that, in moving from isolation into a wider context, requires collaboration and adult interest but also the enthusiasm of the whole school. He sees in other people ideas and sentiments similar to his own, but which are not the product of techniqued silence practice such as mindfulness. This, he suggests, indicates the broad appeal of silence in schools as applied through a variety of avenues.

UK5: ... it's lovely to hear somebody writing about it.

HL: Well it's surprising it's not been done already. But that just shows you maybe how ...

UK5: How rare it is.

HL: ... imagine it is.

UK5: Yeh, yeh, yeh.

HL: Do you get a sense of that?

UK5: Yeh. I think you get the sense of something really happening but you also get a sense of how difficult it is to get it right. Because there's so much, so many ingredients are required. But I would definitely say Helen that we're looking at, I mean my horizon for this is ten to twenty years, even thirty. And it's not something you can force. I think, I think part of it will depend on what happens in the adult world. I think in a sense, for instance with a mindfulness course, if we want people, if we want teachers to teach mindfulness there has to be a relatively significant universe of adult practitioners from whom to draw. I don't know how many teachers are there in the country? 500,000 or something? You know, if we have half a million teachers in the country and only 100,000 of them in the long term. So if there are 500,000 teachers and let's say only 10,000 of them have ever done mindfulness then that imme-diately puts a cap on how it can be actually physically taught in a school. So a lot of what we do in schools is going to depend on what happens culturally in the outside world and in the adult world. It's a limiting factor.

HL: You teach it, but you are also talking about this embodiment thing. And other people I've spoken to who are, you know, these schools I've mentioned, they also embody it. And they talk about the embodiment side of things. Argh! How shall I put this? Why, do you think the ... silence/mindfulness and whatever those practices are that contribute to say strong silence ... do you think it needs to be taught?

UK5: That's a good question. No I mean, it's chicken and egg isn't it? Because I think you might need to teach it in order to set it up. But once it's set up you might not need to teach it. Does that make sense?

HL: It makes sense but I'm ... how does that work?

UK5: Well I think it works by, so, for instance, at the moment at [our school], what I will try and do is I'll have taught all [year ten] and then I'll teach them again the following year hopefully. And what I hope might then happen is that you would have a more accepting audience. So then it might be able to be brought into school assemblies in a way. The Head might refer to it. And ... teach it himself even or embody it more, I don't know. You know, I think there might, I think you might need to do certain things to kickstart it.

I'll tell you a good example we've got here is the anti-bullying culture. I think we have a very, very strong non-bullying, anti-bullying environment here. And part of that was because when we created the anti-bullying system and we had nominated anti-bullying members, boys on the committee and we had some strong characters in the top years leading the way. With the anti-bullying, it needed the campaign, literally a campaign, a kind of marketing campaign within the school. ... the boys made posters about the importance of anti-bullying. And we did a few sort of, well we did quite a lot of creative work to get it into people's heads that it mattered. There was a talk from one of the boys. There were two talks actually from the boys. It created a language, it created a grammar around which one could discuss bullying. And we had representatives etc, etc. And so it did need a kickstart. But once it's been kickstarted it's much easier to ... you can sustain it. And they all understand it and it's implicit and it's embedded in the culture. It could be the same with silence. But the difficult thing is you've really got to be able to persuade people that silence is important. And that's harder. It doesn't have the immediate appeal that anti-bullying does. Kids all know that they hate being teased.

HL: But then what we were talking about earlier to do with a switch or a kick into an awareness of the enjoyment of the whole thing. Do you think that might play a part?

UK5: Yes I think that would play a part. That would take a few years to create because you need all of the kids in the schools to, to understand and appreciate how, how beautiful and nourishing silence can be. ... I still hear about it now from boys I've taught four years ago. They come back and say what they all remembered and how fond they were of it. And, you know, I think, I think it probably is having an effect. The crucial thing is gonna be staff and training. What I'm really excited about is that once people understand what mindfulness is, that it will be entirely non threatening and it will contribute to all that they are doing. You know, poetry and mindfulness come together beautifully. Actually I think it's sort of language and great art which communicate these higher values which silence and stillness help you to experience – help you to connect with.

So I don't think it's impossible but I think almost the stronger the [existing] ethos of the school, the more, the more fiercely ... the harder it is to bring a whole school culture around. ... if you've got a pretty mentally healthy school with a lot of people striving and in the very healthy ways to get kids to really enjoy their subject, you can't impose a culture. It really has to come from belief and understanding. And that takes time. ... the answer for me probably would be to get a series of talks in assembly which are about the importance of stillness and silence, but have different people doing it. So for instance, I'm working very closely with someone in the English department. The Head of sport is passionate about mindfulness in sport. You know there are enough people now, I think, who get it and are prepared to endorse it. But interestingly they are not necessarily 'practitioners'.

One of the most nourishing conversations I've had was with a very experienced English teacher who is also a well known poet and a teacher of creative writing. He doesn't meditate but he has a tremendous understanding of what mindfulness is tapping into, what it delivers. And that's why it's interesting. I think it's somehow trying to put together and articulate this broader set of values which doesn't require any sort of conversion to meditation but which does embrace the values that meditation and mindfulness nurture. ... I'm very confident that silence, stillness, mindfulness could work in any school. I don't think there's any issue there if you've got a Head who believes, staff who understand. And ... an intention to make that work. ... But then you see, something that mitigates probably against it is more the culture in which young people grow up where attention spans are shortened. It's a bit of a cliché but the desire for the immediate image, the immediate song, Youtube on their phones now, constant contact, constant relationships. You know, that idea of being still, I don't think it's the school culture that mitigates against kids learning to be still, I think it's the entertainment culture which does. We're trying to embrace the entertainment culture in the way we explain and teach mindfulness, but it's not easy!

Isolated silence that emerges in schools

Another respondent who had worked in a school with no whole school ethos for silence but who had introduced and encouraged silent reading in his English classrooms, described how silence struck him as both a tangible force of some kind and how it produced an effective outcome for his students; namely the acquisition of reading skills and habits. In conversation with me he joyfully and with obvious fondness called this practice 'Silent Fridays'. This is his account, written upon request, to show how silence can be naturally emergent from a focus on other concerns (here reading competence) and yet still as powerful as deliberate practices.

UK6: A Leavisite English graduate with left leanings, I began teaching in 1976 joining an usual English department in a new (1970) large comprehensive school. At interview, I had been impressed with the contents of the book cupboard that included Tolstoy's *The Cossacks* and a rich variety of what I took to be 'real' literature. The first text I taught to year ten was *The Outsider*, reading it out loud while the group followed, in the department's established manner. I recall, later, reading and teaching Turgenev's *On the Eve* with one year eleven CSE group and *Silas Marner* with another. The department was committed to the idea of sharing examples of high literary culture with its largely working class constituency.

When I arrived at the school, I noticed that many of the year eleven group I taught had an impressive reading profile. I remember two students who had both read Tolstoy and in general the reading profile of the group was formidable. How had this happened? In discussion with colleagues it became clear that certain times of the year students had been given time to read. Much of this had been strongly guided but had also been individualised. Encouraged positively to explore 'real' adult, mature European literature, especially in the form of the novel, these comprehensive school students were reading far beyond their expected horizons, at that time a fashionable sub-canon of ersatz literature. What, I asked, if we did this promotion of reading systematically? What if we used the authority system of the school and the classroom to insist that everybody become a reader and that everybody at least confront the offer of 'quality fiction'?

In my second year of teaching I instituted a practice that the department came to share. It designated one lesson per week out of four as a silent reading lesson, when students would be expected to do nothing apart from read the book they had brought along, usually a book supplied from the school's well-stocked library. As students progressed through the age ranks they would be encouraged to try more demanding fiction, all the time being exposed also to the reading out loud experience indicated briefly above and various other literacy practices that gave high symbolic value, and time, to reading-related activities.

Each class would have a reading record book and each student would have a page in the book to record their reading. Students became habituated to the practice and knew that they would be expected to arrive with a book and would be expected to read through the lesson in silence. When they changed their book it would be recorded in their page in the record book. The teacher would need to strictly supervise the silence of the silent reading, insisting that silence be utterly maintained. Usually the class would settle into a self-managed silence. The role of the teacher, as I saw it, in this scenario was to be a fellow-reader. So the teacher would sit down at the teacher's desk at the front with a book with the intention of reading along with the group.

I can't claim to have invented this, since it corresponded with some practices already established in the department and had been informed by what I had heard about and read about USSR (universal sustained silent reading) that had been advocated through the 1960s. But I became committed to it and sought to formalise the reading lesson as an absolutely essential weekly event for every pupil doing English – which meant every student from year seven to eleven and a significant number beyond.

I followed this practice for seventeen years as a full time English teacher. Later in my career I tended to organise the reading lesson for Fridays, so that often all my Friday lessons would be given over to collective silent reading. There is no question about the success of this method in the production of readers. Students subjected to this regime for several years became readers to a significant degree and in a significant number of cases became readers of the favoured 'quality fiction' or 'literature'.

One significant, but difficult to define, dimension of this practice was that it was frequently the case that the whole class, once settled into silent reading, would achieve an intensely quiet mood of concentration. At these often sustained moments the sensation of quiet was highly charged and seemed to have a positive emotional quality that it was hard to define or even to describe. Few experiences in professional life have the intensity and the strong satisfaction of that experience. I always had the feeling that that positive charge was shared by the group, that the group revelled in its silence and that they too valued the shared experience of intense focused silence for itself. And of course one of the important features of this activity is that it wasn't related to 'outcomes' nor to 'schemes of work' nor to any planned progression of learning nor educational targets.

There is now a well-established practice of sustained silent reading that is particularly practiced in primary schools where the division of time and space is more open. For a researched account of this practice and the production of readers, see West, A. (1986) 'The Production of Readers' in *The English Magazine*, London: ILEA English Centre, no. 17, Autumn, pp4-9.

Conclusion

Both these teacher accounts of silence practices give a sense of something special happening. Silence in schools is certainly not ordinary. Even without a context of a whole school ethos, individual and isolated practice within otherwise un-silence-focused schools brings benefit. This benefit is seen as definitely evolving out of the silence itself.

The road to bringing silence into a school does seem to be ordinary or familiar. It attaches itself to activities and expectations that are already very significantly part of the grammar of a school: the classroom, the teacher, the lesson. These are remarkably stable features of schooling (Tyack and Cuban, 1995). Silence is unlikely to change that grammar in terms of the look of a school.

Without a whole school ethos, silence relies on individuals who champion it. Are these special and unusual people with a talent for silence, to be able to be with, and work with and in silence? Whether schools and silence can only mix because of such people is an interesting question. If society as a whole were more used to silence as an everyday concept, silence in schools would need to rely less on champions to introduce it. It would be more normal and possibly used with greater frequency by more people. For silence in schools to become mainstreamed in this way might require wider society to understand it first, so that it can develop as a regular feature or idea of schooling 'grammar' or logic –

whether or not an underpinning philosophy is in place. The under-pinning would come instead from outside the school. Silence could possibly enter society with such impact that it affects schools in this way, but until this happens practice for silence starts in schools through specialist enthusiasts who incorporate it in their pedagogical practice.

In this chapter, as in the last, we see the art of silence in schools. It does not seem however that silence might function and operate in only certain types of school or with only certain members of staff in the schools. There is no suggestion that silence is exclusive, suiting only well resourced schools. It does however seem to require interest, enthusiasm and commitment for its richer elements to emerge. The art is to open up the creative educational possibilities schools can access to a particular kind of experience and atmosphere.

4
The different forms of
silence in schools

Introduction

There are as many forms of silence to be found in schools as there are forms of silence to be found in life as a whole. As Foucault says, simply, but also with great complexity: 'There is not one but many silences' (1998:27).

Although the ordinary ubiquity yet diversity of silence is in every school, I wish to make a 'mark in the sand' about the concept of silence for school use. In what follows I identify schools as operating with two main types of silence, of which I consider only one to be silence. To qualify to be a silence the form must be strong. I claim that what I call 'weak silence' is 'nonsilence' – not silence.

This chapter argues that silence in schools ought never to be weak. Weak silence is a negative version that ought to be stripped of its status as a silence because silence ought to be a beneficial feature of the school.

There is plenty of talk about such weak silence and its detrimental effects in school settings. I offer a brief overview of the literature that discusses this but the main body of the discussion which follows concerns strong silence as silence proper and argues that it is theoretically positive silence only which can bring change that is enhancing to schools.

Silence is outside binary systems that make distinctions between weak and strong (Kalamaras, 1994). It is beyond language in terms of discourse (spoken or written), yet has a powerful part to play in functions of language (see eg. Dauenhauer, 1980). But this radical refusal of silence to submit to human demarcations can also, happily, be ignored. It is both possible and useful to artificially ring-fence silence as a concept, so as to make it a tool for human understanding and benefit. Firmly grasping the conceptual slipperiness of silence (Schwartz, 1996) is to invite a willing friend into one's house. Submitting to its power to elude human demarcations, where 'what we cannot speak about we must pass over in silence' (Wittgenstein, 1993:74) is, paradoxically, a part of this friendly and useful exchange: not knowing; not being able to say; not understanding through and with discourse has purpose.

Weak silence

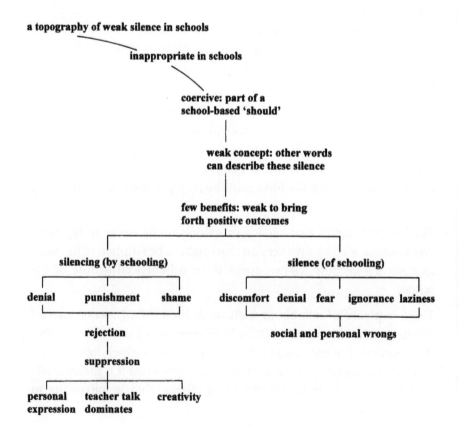

A certain negative form of silence has become a generalised technology of education: it is seen as a necessary tool for control and maintenance of existing hierarchies and power relationships. Such silence is actively used by schools as a system. The use depends on the nature of the education, the management of the school as a community and the desired educational outcomes. Too much use of silence, in negative ways that involve unequal power relations results in weak educational situations. Unfortunately the use of negative silence in schools is common. Research on weak silence in schools observes that it is a problem:

> Silencing as a disciplinary act reveals and sustains imbalanced power relationships between individuals and between groups. The state of silence indeed signifies a state of oppression. (Huey-li, 2001:161)

Weak silence has not received much attention from writers on education who have a sense of strong silence, with the exception of Moira Von Wright and Deborah Orr, who both understand both kinds of silence (von Wright, 2008; Orr, 2002). Generally, however, weak silences are discussed separately from discussions of strong silence, as a type of silence that needs to be changed. The idea of silence as transformable is not often considered. The negativity of weak silence is commented upon as a concrete issue in a great deal of literature (eg. Fine, 1987; Walkerdine, 1985; Castagno, 2008; Gilmore, 1985). The various forms that these school silences take have been described as: denial, oppression, domination, fear, marginalisation, and so on. They are manifestations of wider social problems in schools such as homophobia, sexism and racism (Sillin, 2005; Castagno, 2008; Gilligan and Brown, 1993). Where writers identify weak silences as a systemic *function* of school education (even if indirectly, eg. Harber, 2004; Peim and Flint, 2012), one can even become enraged by weak silence in schools.

However, this book is chiefly concerned with the positivity of silence and so the section on weak silence in schools is brief, despite the strong emotions the issue can elicit. Forms of silence in schools are not necessarily connected to authority or hierarchies, nor is authority in schools necessarily bad. It can be managed in relational ways that are productive or 'good enough' (Bingham, 2008). When researching for this book with schools which have worked with silence over long periods of time, it was a surprise to discover how strong silence appears to play a role in creating naturally emerging democratic elements which work well alongside authority in schools. It appears to transform what might have the power to be negative and coercive into something relationally and productively interpersonal. More research is needed on whether this is indeed happening and just how these effects of what I would describe as love, translated through authority, emerge. What in one school is an abuse of power is found to be useful in another school because it feels different.

The dynamic interplay of silences shows the possible power of silence in a school to change its environment towards greater fairness for all. Moreover, silence as a whole is a responsive underpinning for all experience, responding according to the attitude brought to it. Using silence to gain power over people brings negative results, whereas using it to develop their powers creates positivity. The relationship of the individual to silence determines the kind of silence manifest in the school. This relationship shapes how it functions educationally for good or not. Negative silence takes certain forms:

- coercion
- teacher talk dominating
- avoiding discussion of difficult or controversial topics
- seeing chosen silence as dysfunctional

Silence as coercion

Forcing people to be silent creates a bad situation:

> Teachers who scream for silence, who threaten and punish children into silent submission, will never know a lasting silence or silence that is filled with thoughtfulness. Lurking within the forced silence is a scream of resistance. (Clair, 1998:25)

People who do not want to be still and quiet and have things to say create tensions with those who want stillness and quiet. People are not in harmony when they are compelled to do things against their will and without having any say. They tolerate, ignore, rebel, sulk, retreat from the coercion or kick at it (Marsh *et al*, 1978; Gilmore, 1985; Carlen *et al*, 1992; Yoneyama, 1999). No state of harmony is possible. Coercion precludes co-operation, dialogue or seeking to understand, thus a silence about the silence is imposed.

Busy teachers in schools might say: 'But what choice do we have with 30 children to control? We need to get the work done and get the results'. The dynamics around behaviour, teacher time and effort, league tables and so on can make coercive silence seem a necessity. But there are those who argue that such coercive factors take schools from their proper educational purposes (eg. Biesta, 2009; Gribble, 2001; Neill, 1936; Olson, 2009; Miller, 2008). Silence that is coerced fails to engage with the long term work of schooling as a dialogic environment. Such silence is oppression (Orr, 2002); it is more about power than education (Friere, 1972; Fine, 1987). As Maria Montessori observed: 'In ordinary schools it is always thought that silence is to be obtained by command' (1990:139).

The style of education where educational delivery is managed through authority and 'educational' plays of power 'permeate[s] classroom life so primitively' that it can 'shut down the very voices of students and their communities that public education claims to nurture' (Fine, 1987: 158). A coercive 'educational' silence is used to control or manipulate circumstances: the stare, the sharp pregnant pause, the look, the subtle movement of a hand. This is not silence – it is control.

Teacher talk

Here teacher-talk is allowed to dominate (Chaudron, 1988). Students understand that silence is generally the appropriate mode for them (Jaworski and Sachdev, 1998). Seen from an emancipatory and critical pedagogic perspective this is silencing by an omission to develop forms of voiced 'literariness' (Friere, 1972). The teacher is colluding with students who know the passive drill. Overturning this dynamic is difficult for both teachers and students, even if both parties would prefer to be speaking in conversation. Traditional methods of pedagogic delivery in many schools cause silence to function in a way that shuts down the students, whilst demanding of the teacher a monologic style (Fuller and Snyder, 1991; Hayes and Matusov, 2005; Leander, 2002). Silence becomes an educational intruder. It is a threat to educational order and it resists any freedom of voice (Lewis, 2010). In such an atmosphere silence has no validation as being a way of knowing that is communicative and useful (Kalamaras, 1994). The naturalised, although constructed, authoritarian mode means that students must be silent and silenced for much of their classroom experience (Meighan *et al*, 2007: 65-76).

The teacher in authority feels they need not only pre-determine how conversations go for the sake of learning, but often begins any conversation with the answer in mind, ready or primed to show the ignorant student their ability to teach the 'truth' and how their own knowledge is superior. This silences students and stifles their curiosity, their discovery for themselves, and the wonder of no one really *knowing* in advance what is to be learnt (Hayes and Matusov, 2005).

When conversation ensues, it is often spontaneous: one of the students defies the circumscribed behaviour and expectations. Such occurrences should be sustained but this is hard work when the standard mode of interaction is the antithesis of open-ended conversation between genuinely interested individuals.

Silencing can inhibit peers who would like to speak out. Children can contain other children they wish to have power over. Boys deliberately silence girls (Leander, 2002). Similarly, students who are 'othered' are marginalised in silent spaces – physical, mental, emotional, social – because of their sexuality, gender (Gilligan and Brown, 1993; Curtis, 2008; Fontaine, 1997), race (Bloom, 2009) or special educational needs (Maddern, 2009). Staff in some schools operate in a similar way.

Don't talk about it

Topics may be silenced that warrant discussion, such as sex (Begoray and Bannister, 2008), sexuality (Thornton, 2004), abortion rights, human rights, work-place rights, abuse, violence or money. Deliberately avoiding these issues because they are sensitive or controversial could be harmful.

Large scale silences which do not permit a range of opinions are weak. They are exclusive and excluding, not encompassing and inclusive. The National Curriculum can determine what is silenced. A National Curriculum review in 2011 advised that the topic of climate change in the science curriculum since 1995, for example be removed (Shepherd, 2011).

Elected silence seen as a threat or overlooked

Millions of silences are created by schools for individuals but these are rarely desired. Many children's unique experience and personal contribution to schools are ignored, denied or replaced with weak silences (Harber, 2004). This happens for many reasons, not all of them malign. The possibility of real voice is caught up in a complex web of the power, exclusions, permissions, traditions and controls which weaken the prospect of the child's voice being heard. Sometimes that voice might be wordless: an elected silence as a form of communication of self opinion. But that also is lost (Lewis, 2010; von Wright, 2008). Chosen silence is not understood or recognised in education and this creates coerced silence. Children feel pressured to 'speak up' even when they might not wish to do so, for example about their emotions in circle time (Ecclestone and Hayes, 2009).

Teachers may sabotage children's elected silences deliberately, through clumsiness or perhaps by professional imperatives they feel require them to do so (Ollin, 2008). When children express themselves through strong silence, through a love of stillness for example, this may be seen as a threat and met with disapproval.

In her analysis of a child who wanted to be quiet in class but was stalked by teachers eager to make him perform and 'show interest', Von Wright speaks of the difficulty of getting a balance within the asymmetry of the teacher-pupil power relation (von Wright, 2012). She argues that silence of an elected kind seems to be no longer an option in schools and is seen as pathological:

- We want to help you, but you have to come half way first, the teacher Anne declared to the student Bob.
- I do not wish to be helped, Bob responded.
- But you have to be more active in class, and if you know the answers you have to show me that you know, Anne said.
- Why?
- Because that is what school is about ... (*op cit*)

Von Wright points out that students like Bob, who elect to be silent, might be making a choice they feel is right for them. For a school system to demand that he conform to what they say is educational interferes in this choice, by 'blocking the student's path to the world' (*op cit*) through disapproval of the method of educational journeying chosen and taken by a student. This is not an educational exchange but a fight over form.

Similarly, government agendas around *Every Child a Talker* (DCSF, 2008) and other initiatives to get children to be verbally loquacious do not seem to recognise that not every child might want to be a talker, and might have valid and important reasons for that:

> ... it is in this context [of mass and multi-media communication] that a kind of sociability and apparent openness is promoted, and this again is understood in terms of the nomenclature of skills – as interpersonal or social, communication or entrepreneurial. If these are seen as virtuous, the inclinations to isolate oneself or to remain silent are regarded less as vices than as weaknesses, as tendencies to be overcome on the path to confidence and self-awareness. (Blake *et al*, 2000:146)

Rogers (2000) gives a psychological example of a choice to be silent in his account of therapeutic sessions with a boy who has difficulties in his family life and who never spoke until he suddenly asked one day:

> *Dick:* How much time do I have left?
>
> *Therapist:* Seven minutes, Dick
>
> *Dick:* I might as well rock for a while. (*He goes and sits in the rocking-chair. He closes his eyes and quietly rocks.*) How much time do I have left now?
>
> *Therapist:* Five more minutes, Dick.
>
> *Dick: (sighs very deeply):* Ah, five more minutes *all to myself.* (p246)

The failure to appreciate that, in school, silence can function as an important chosen educational space for the self, will mean that all silence is defined weak.

A bridge between weak and strong silence

In the West, the dominance of Cartesian rationality as a framework of thought does not allow for silence to be anything other than what Kalamaras calls 'annihilation' (1994:61). Western thinkers tend to perceive silence as *anything* negative which lacks discourse. This is a serious limitation on engagement with silence; it stops proper access to it. Kalamaras suggests this negative aspect to the signifier silence is a western misinterpretation of what silence is. Western thought lacks a holistic perspective often involving paradox – which is common in Eastern thinking – which would enable it to conceive of a mode of knowing (to include knowing silence), that does not need to form itself through conceptual oppositions. Nonconceptual knowing of silence is not easily understandable to a western mind. This is not a lack of knowing silence or a failure of knowing. It is a different way of knowing.

In eastern thought, silence is seen as a mode of non-conceptual knowing, involving intuition and a juxtaposition of possibly contrasting and contradictory ideas. It is an active principle and this is itself a way of knowing (op cit). Silence is not only present and tangible but works with a human mind to enlighten it, to enhance its capacities and make life and living more real and truthful. Silence is identified as a something.

In contrast to eastern views of naming silence as something, most schooling commonly names nothing as a silence, as when an absence of voice is called a silence (Fine, 1987; Leander, 2002; Huey-li, 2001). We could call this oppression through lack of voice or, 'voicelack'.

I maintain that silence in schools should be the strong kind because only the strong kind is positive and is truly silence. The weak form is voicelack, shutting-up, power-abuse, asymmetrical-voice, waste, oppression, refusal ... There are other ways to name these situations than by using the word 'silence'. If silence in schools is consistently understood as having both weak and strong forms, then it is difficult to do this.

It is more useful to identify silence as one thing actively happening in schools, and disregard western binary frameworks of thinking. In the rest of the book, when I discuss silence I refer to silence that is strong enough to bring benefits.

(Strong) silence

Other writers have different words for positive silences. Dauenhauer (1980), for instance, writes thus of 'deep' silence: 'deep silence is encountered as the silence which pervades utterance ... it appears not to flow but abide' (op cit:21). Zembylas and Michaelides (2004) refer to 'contemplative' silence, which 'nourishes creativity, passion and wonder lying at the heart of all significant learning and living' (p209). Ephratt (2008) identifies a connected form of silence he calls 'eloquent', which he characterises as 'part of communication, as the speaker choosing, when

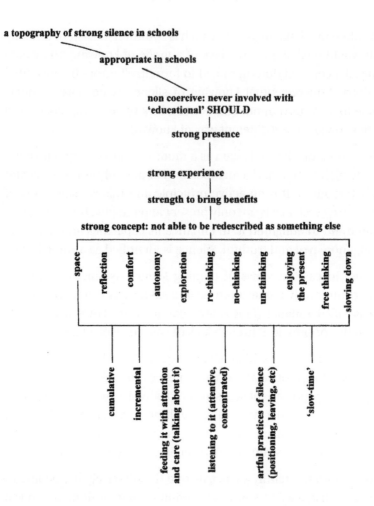

it is his or her turn, to express himself or herself by silence' (p1911). Bruneau (1973) uses the idea of 'slow-time', meaning a form of silence allowing 'inner time' for the individual to 'think, absorb and reflect' (Ollin, 2008:268).

I argue that a school ethos can be imbued with all these qualities: intimacy, contemplation, a slowness allowing reflection. However, I encompass also a deliberate effort on the part of the educationists, including the children, in the school to cultivate and develop a sense of silence as an atmosphere, a culture, an 'ecology', as UK5 called it. Silence of this kind makes demands on the approach of a school to knowledge: other pathways than the purely cognitive merge and flourish. Being embraced by silence in a school, content to dwell in silence and not afraid to be a part of what it can offer is a solid experience. To know and appreciate the concept is to be with the experience. Such silence is tangible; it is in the air. As we saw in chapter two, the schools whose practice with silence is long term and all-embracing have achieved a sense and an experience of strong/deep/contemplative/slow silence. Furthermore, the silence has become educational in that it benefits the education offered.

A positive psychology

The next chapter describes work that is going on in schools relating to silence which aims to be beneficial to the children and staff. However, there are questions about the benefits of (strong) silence in schools. For instance, when a 'movement' for positive psychology in education is growing and cannot be denied (Kristjansson, 2010), do educationists wary of such interventions need to add the phenomenon of silence to their list of positive psychology interventions in schools? Is silence in schools a form of positive psychology? I suggest it is and is not. It satisfies the key concept of positive psychology as involved with happiness and enhancing well-being. But it is not an intervention. It requires commitment and dialogic, democratic conditions, time, patience and a relationship with silence. Other aspects of positive psychology are enmeshed in the effects of power of epistemic discourse such as society creates to order but also to exclude (Foucault, 1977, 2002, 2004). Positive psychology interventions into school settings have been problematised for not acknowledging these aspects (Ecclestone and Hayes, 2009; Suissa, 2008).

Silence, on the other hand, is a 'pathway' to happiness (Seligman, 2002) because practising silence regularly improves mood (Williams *et al*, 2007). But it cannot be quantifiably or even qualitatively assessed as effective, as positive psychology seeks to do.

Mindfulness and meditation are currently being assessed in scientific ways (eg. Huppert and Johnson, 2010). This is good for silence in schools because it provides a valuable evidence base but this is not the whole story. Sometimes practicing with silence in schools can make one unhappy because it is part of a complex personal journey towards a less encumbered state of mind, with less rumination. Eventually the journey will bring one to greater quietude and inner peace. Measures and concerns for effectiveness are helpful but they are not the journey.

Educational silence

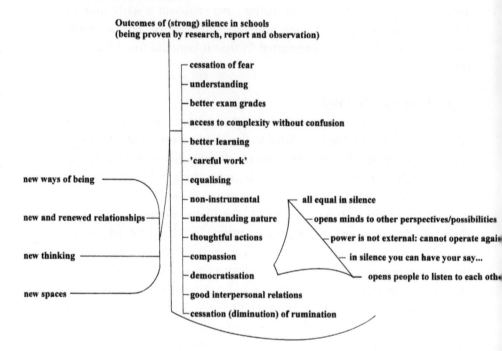

Outcomes of (strong) silence in schools
(being proven by research, report and observation)

- cessation of fear
- understanding
- better exam grades
- access to complexity without confusion
- better learning
- 'careful work'

new ways of being
- equalising
- non-instrumental

new and renewed relationships
- understanding nature
- thoughtful actions

new thinking
- compassion
- democratisation

new spaces
- good interpersonal relations
- cessation (diminution) of rumination

- all equal in silence
- opens minds to other perspectives/possibilities
- power is not external: cannot operate again
- in silence you can have your say...
- opens people to listen to each other

In educational settings silence is created not just through techniques such as meditation and mindfulness but also by educational means. In schools where weak silences do not predominate, silence flourishes and coercion and dominant teacher talk are avoided. Difficult or controversial topics are discussed as dysfunctional. Such schools utilise a different *modality* of education than schools that have the problems of 'weak silence', such as poor interpersonal relationships (eg. bullying) or a lack of openness and silences of denial about difficult issues. A modality is, in my meaning here, a world of theory and practice. A school which uses a whole school Meeting (see Fielding, 2010; Neill, 1968) to regulate the school is a democratic environment and community such as Summerhill School in Suffolk or Sands School in Devon, Sudbury Valley School in Massachusetts, USA and others around the world (Sudbury Valley School, 1992; Bennis and Graves, 2007; Neill,

70

1968; Gribble, 2001; Appleton, 2002). Such schools exhibit more features of silence than non-democratic schools, without having specific silence practices.

Schools of democratic practice are reported by those involved as places of freedom, respect and joy (Stronach and Piper, 2008; Appleton, 2002; Goodsman, 1992; Curry, 1947; Schwartz and Maher, 2006) – qualities identified as outcomes of silence practices in education (Patten, 1997; Erricker and Erricker, 2001).

I believe that silence should come first and democracy will follow. UK2 illustrates that the modality of school does not need to be democratic first: silence takes it towards the educational, understood as dialogic. This line of flight can offer educational experiences with a sense of personal and social purpose (Biesta, 2010; Blake *et al*, 2000) whatever the modality of the school.

Elective home education of an autonomous style which allows freedom of curriculum content and pace of learning, also fosters freedom, interpersonal harmony and joy. The modality of choosing how and what one learns generates silence features. Feeling at ease and being able to relax into a sense of quietude – outcomes of silence practices – also feature in autonomous style home education (Thomas and Pattison, 2007; Dowty, 2000).

A school with silent features might look wild and noisy to those not in tune with what distinguishes it – the alpha-wave brain states in the community. These can be adduced through educational signs such as absorption in a chosen task and self-reported satisfaction with learning engagement. For instance:

> I like how I've learned, I like who I am, and I like what I know ... I'm going to like to be like whoever I end up being. (Sheffer, 1995:97)

This home educated student did not report silence practice, but she had the freedom of decisions about educational pacing and she speaks happily and confidently about her education in the same spirit as those who engage with silence. In schools with techniqued silence practices such as meditation, reports are for more efficient education:

> The findings of the research suggested that profound positive changes occurred in the cognitive capacity of the children due to the meditation pro-

cess. Training the mind in the art of attention/concentration would seem to lead to a shift in the quality of engagement in the learning process, and therefore a shift in the capacity to learn. (Mann, 2001b:43)

Silence techniques also reduce stress in teachers' professional practice (Anderson *et al*, 1999; Winzelberg and Luskin, 1999; Gold *et al*, 2009). Purposeful, personally meaningful and satisfying education becomes imbued with the spirit of silence for creativity and exploration (Lane, 2006).

Other ways of building a culture of silence for education

Ways of quiet considering are being promoted in schools by organisations such as SAPERE and the Institute for the Advancement of Philosophy for Children to improve young people's reflection and reasoning skills (Topping and Trickey, 2007; Trickey and Topping, 2004), across the age range (Echeverria and Hannam, 2009).

Self-managed measures such as personalised and autonomous time management (Paludan, 2006) are a part of a silent school culture. For instance, children who prefer to get up late can manage their energy in ways which contribute to efficient learning (Kelley, 2008). Reflecting the biological rhythm of the body is a path towards an inner relaxation that can become a silent state of mind. A culture or aesthetics of silence in schools is a basic prerequisite for the idea of 'art of the self'. This fits with making oneself up as one goes along, described by Foucault as an important attitude and 'technology' of care achieved through mechanisms such as keeping a reflective journal (Foucault, 1986; 1988). If becoming and being through education is mixed with being and becoming peaceful, contented and a member of a collective society (Biesta, 2008), then the 'empty hands' of silence can help facilitate education. A school culture that is emptied by silence in its midst loses only a sedimented, already given world. This leaves a blank canvas on which to recreate, re-imagine and innovate – an important imperative for education and its future (Alexander, 2009; Children Schools and Families Committee, 2010; Lawn and Furlong, 2011).

Extremes of silence as part of the package

The phenomenon of silence is also connected to mystical experiences of the sublime and the other-worldly (see eg. Picard, 2002; Kenny, 2011;

Theresa of Avila, 2004). Extreme, ineffable, 'absolute' silence is not a concern for schools. Children can, instead, get to know silence better through regular discussion of its nature and small scale experiences in a school setting, as the headteachers describe in chapter two. Although extreme experiences of silence are unlikely, students and teachers are naturally poised to experience something of wonder and awe in their daily actions and understandings (Zembylas and Michaelides, 2004; Caranfa, 2004). Learning is about discovery and discovery involves awe. Thomas S. Kuhn explains what is possible in the way of awe through new understanding:

> Suddenly the fragments in my head sorted themselves out in a new way, and fell into place together. My jaw dropped, for all at once Aristotle seemed a very good physicist indeed, but of a sort I'd never dreamed possible. (Kuhn, 2000:16)

As a small moment of outwardly silent but inwardly active understanding, Kuhn's words suggest that different forms of wonderful silence are possible: whole school silence; inwardly experienced wondering awareness; inter-relational moments of bonding and connection; awe and wonder at discoveries of learning. These all form part of the whole that is silence in school settings. The experiences of silence manifest in ways that are not prescriptive or predictable, from degrees of ineffable awareness to simple and almost unnoticeable mental peace and calm.

Silence as relative absence of noise

Silence is a state of mind, independent of sound and not necessarily connected to responses towards the world. However, it helps the state of mind of silence to flourish if noise levels in school buildings are low. Such silence is a democratic creation and should be seen as within the context of the school. It is a quality not a quantity.

In a school environment loud noise would be anathema (Clay, 2009). But although government guidelines (*Building Bulletin 93*) were set, parents, teachers and organisations have complained that the Building Schools for the Future initiative showed little respect for noise management. According to the National Deaf Children's Society (NDCS, 2009a) some new builds have been shown not to comply with *Building Bulletin 93*. This organisation observes that: 'Specific concerns include: No requirement to test the acoustics of a newly built school pre-completion in Building Bulletin 93 or elsewhere. DCSF have not conducted any central monitoring or quality assurance checks of acoustics' (NDCS, 2009b).

All children lose out in schools when noise levels make learning difficult. Those who are hard of hearing suffer especially. Acoustic management in schools can directly adversely affect reading levels and language ability for any child (Haines *et al*, 2001; Lundquist *et al*, 2000), and even induce forms of helplessness (Maxwell and Evans, 2000).

Acoustics which are badly designed for engaging with learning instructions or muting high volume communal chatter cause problems. The structure of the building of certain schools can even amplify noise (Lundquist *et al*, 2000; Maxwell and Evans, 2000). Even where there are potentially strongly silent spaces in schools, some are being appropriated by consumerist advertising in schools which sign contracts that stipulate that a specific TV channel be watched (Apple, 1995). Some commentators argue that this kind of noise is vandalism against the good life (Sim, 2007; Prochnik, 2010; Maitland, 2008; Hempton and Grossman, 2009). Yet there is little official assessment of school noise levels. Studies do, however, (eg. Lundquist *et al*, 2000; Maxwell and Evans, 2000) show noise levels in some schools to exceed the level condoned by World Health Organisation guidelines: below 50-55 dB(A) (WHO, 1999).

In seeking quietude and practicing to that end for inner calm, people in a school setting would naturally regulate noise levels rather than disregard its possible detrimental affects. They become aware that:

UK2: ... when you're mediating, when you're silent, your listening is very acute isn't it, your hearing is very acute at a sensory level and deeper and that then would be available to you in ordinary everyday life. You're attentive to what's going on and when you speak, you're aware of the sound of your voice, the effect of the sound of your voice. So, I suppose what I'm saying is that the meditative practice heightens our awareness of the human apparatus and how to use it.

Conclusion

Silence is a fundamental sub-structure of life (Dauenhauer, 1980). What I mean by silence in schools entails stillness, quiet, peace, calm, attentiveness, absence of rumination, awareness, intuitive appreciation. It is beneficial and allows educational activity and purpose to flourish: 'Proper education and proper teaching are based on the substance of silence' (Picard, 2002:69).

Silence, if embedded in a school, softens authoritarianisms and fosters democratic features, as I discuss in chapter six.

Educational silence is a new concept. Understanding how it works or might work in schools is only beginning. It is being variously named: eg. 'contemplative pedagogy' (eg. Hart, 2004) or 'silent pedagogy' (Ollin, 2008). I have named it 'silence' but as underpinned by a theoretical framework which excludes weak silences in schools.

Silence in schools will no doubt attract other labels and theoretical frameworks as the thinking evolves but what thinkers about contemplative or silent pedagogical forms and atmospheres seem to believe in is its educational power.

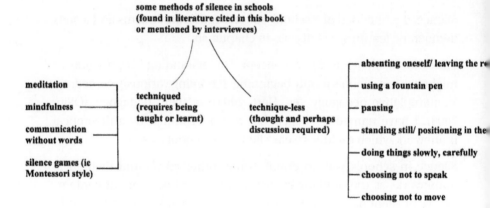

some methods of silence in schools
(found in literature cited in this book
or mentioned by interviewees)

meditation

mindfulness

communication
without words

silence games (ie
Montessori style)

techniqued
(requires being
taught or learnt)

technique-less
(thought and perhaps
discussion required)

absenting oneself/ leaving the r●

using a fountain pen

pausing

standing still/ positioning in the●

doing things slowly, carefully

choosing not to speak

choosing not to move

5

Silence as practiced
in schools

UK2: ... but the term 'meditation' is like the term 'dyslexia'. It's an umbrella term and people mean many things by it. That may also apply to the word silence ...

Introduction

There is too much going on to discuss here all the activities for meditation, mindfulness and deliberate introduction of silence practices into schools around the world. The 'field almost seems to have exploded ...' (Hastings and Singh, 2010:132). Enthusiasm for silence in many domains, not just schooling, is spreading internationally. There has always been interest in silence. Silence in cultural, interpersonal and social terms is often defined by national norms of behaviour which differ from country to country (see eg. Tannen and Saville-Troike, 1995; Yoneyama, 1999). In educational terms, it is new. But although world-wide, silence does not seem to be nationally determined as an elected school practice.

All human beings have an ability to be in silence and to have, or develop, a silent state of mind, a 'mindset, a philosophy, a meaning context to the practice' (Garrison Institute, 2008:3). This is not cultural but rather physiological, psychological, emotional and even spiritual, and can be experienced in the same way around the world. It will be interesting to see whether silence practices in schools develop integral cultural differences in time but so far there are no national differences.

77

Therefore, when this book discusses what is happening in the UK, similar activities can also be happening elsewhere. Silence is about nature, although access to it can be nurtured in schools. Issues of 'contemplative education' practices are 'an emergent research field or body of methodology' in the United States too, where the issues in this book are also under discussion (see Garrison Institute, 2008:1-5).

New philanthropic organisations are working specifically in this area, such as the David Lynch Foundation (meditation) and the (Goldie) Hawn Foundation (mindfulness). They are raising the profile of silence practices for schooling in the popular imagination, through web presence especially. Scientific research into understanding the effects of silence practices such as meditation and mindfulness with children and teachers is making an impact in international academic circles, because the results overwhelmingly show that they are of benefit. The interviews in chapter two where a whole school ethos for silence has formed, point towards this. Headteachers are beginning to understand and use silence and are reporting that it is worthwhile (eg. Woman's Hour, 2011; Paton, 2011).

Silence in schools through techniqued practices such as meditation and mindfulness is growing. The voices advocating silence in schools can back up their claims with scientific evidence and teachers and parents are listening to what silence in schools can mean for their children. The phenomenon is slowly acquiring credibility and respect, despite occasional challenges. A recent spat in the letters section of the *Times Educational Supplement* showed that some saw the expansion of Maharishi schools to three and possibly more schools (Rogers, 2011a)

Krishnamurti Schools

Krishnamurti schools around the world adopt silence as a part of their educational ethos (Hunter, 1988). At the independent (co-ed) **Brockwood Park School** in Hampshire a meeting is held before breakfast each day. Those attending sit in the Assembly Hall for ten minutes in quietude. Jiddu Krishnamurti spoke of the need for 'special places for silence' in the heart of a school (Forbes, 2000). As well as the eight or so Krishnamurti Foundation schools around the world, other schools are inspired by Krishnamurti teachings on education.

Quaker schools

Quaker schools in the UK have a long and integral history of the use of silence:

> Every day, at all seven Quaker schools in the UK, there are several deliberate periods of communal silence: the beginning and end of assembly, and before the start of meals. But at least once a week, as well, the whole school gathers for Meeting, when, for as long as 15 minutes, everyone is left to their thoughts ... What students use the silence for is up to them, but it has a profound impact on how they conduct themselves around the school. (McCormack, 2008)

At the silent meetings, the participants sit in a square so that everyone is equal. Not all the pupils in these schools are Quakers. Julie Lodrick, the Principal of the independent Quaker girls **The Mount School** in York, describes the Quaker principles towards silence and silent practice as 'grounding' for the children (Barker, 2009).

as a threat to scientific rigour. A letter protested that such schools engaged in 'pseudoscience', because they spoke of transcendental meditation as transforming 'consciousness' (Thompson, 2011).

Practices for silence are here to stay, however, backed by the scientifically researched evidence (eg. Burke, 2010; Huppert and Johnson, 2010) and possibly also the rise of 'positive psychology' (Kristjansson, 2010) and 'therapeutic education' initiatives (Ecclestone and Hayes, 2009) which are including silence in schools. Katherine Weare, a proponent of Social Emotional Learning (SEL), for example, suggests silence might be used in school-based interventions (2010).

There is a danger that, because of powerful benefits, silence and its practices may get ensnared in a complex web of 'educational' interventions, solutions, improvements, business models and so on.

I want to stress that silence practices in schools are part of a baseline but that silence itself is the thing for education (see chapter seven). The goal is achievement of silent states of mind and a silent-tending atmosphere. Practices are part of the journey that silence in one's life introduces. Interested practitioners react to silence in schools by becoming inspired and amazed, moved and encouraged by what they see. Silence is in tune

---

Schools using mindfulness as a practice

Various state and public schools in the UK have used meditation programmes of 'student sitting' to positive effect (Levete, 2001c) or short programmes of mindfulness, such as at the independent boys **Tonbridge School** in Kent under the direction of Richard Burnett (Burnett, 2009) or a similar course run at the independent boys **Hampton School** in Middlesex.

---

with their vocation as educationists, not just another school improvement intervention. Take for example the reaction by someone to a talk I gave on aspects of this book and the idea of freely allowing a child to stare out the window. He told me I had reminded him why he entered education in the first place. Another suggested that what silence in schools touches upon is opening an educational Pandora's box that needs to be opened. Silence for education is a topic that inspires passion for good school practice. Silence requires a dialogic, caring, people-oriented approach, as reflected in the testimonies of the interviewees in chapters two and three.

Silence practice initiatives are the detail, but silence itself is complicated: it is in a profoundly involved sense about people (see eg. Picard, 2002; Maitland, 2008; Sim, 2007; Forrest, 2010; Clair, 1998; Hall *et al*, 1997; Haskins, 2010; Brown and Coles, 2008). Silence in a school is demanding, resistant, stubborn, fragile, flexible, able, slow, effective and much else. It does not comply with human demands for results. Although it does deliver the potential for schools to be better businesses it does so incidentally. Because it is outside logical conceptual binary thinking where stable identification is easy to impose, silence escapes identification. Yet it is simple, cost-free but valuable. It is accessible to all, independent of socio-economic status or factors such as race, gender and physical capacities. As 'a zero signifier with a zero signified' (Kurzon, 1998:9), silence is a negation of any understanding because it does not point to any sign and has no sign. All we can see of it are its effects. This is unusual in a modern world where signs of fashion, performance and display are powerful (Baudrillard, 1993). For school children obsessed with the latest branded gear, an experience without signs is an escape and a release.

Techniqued silence

For some years, forward thinking educationists have been championing the use of meditative practices in classrooms for practical reasons and also for the educationally productive intrigue that silence creates. *Meditation in Schools: calmer classrooms*, brought together different authors with experience of successful practice, researched qualitatively:

> ... to show how meditation can contribute to specific school and curriculum activities, and enhance learning and educational provision generally with students of different ages and abilities. Emphasis is also placed on the enhancement of student's well-being. Meditation is a way to help develop the positive potential of the mind and heart. In educational terms it enables both cognitive and affective development. It can radically enhance student's enjoyment of their learning and their ownership of it. For the teacher, it can significantly change the school and classroom environment in which he or she works. (Erricker and Erricker, 2001)

In the last decade scientific research trials, concerning techniqued silence practices for and with education have created an 'emergent field where ... the research is still in its infancy' (Burke, 2010:133). Exploration of silence in schools is at the beginning of achieving mainstream acceptance, although this seems to be happening unusually fast.

Are meditative practices with children in a variety of clinical, therapeutic and institutional settings, including schools, diverse in nature and appli-

---

A little bit of silence...

A meditation programme was introduced into 31 Catholic schools in one diocese in Queensland, Australia in 2006 which engaged more than 10,000 students between the ages of 5 and 18 years. The objective of the study was to conduct an initial evaluation of this meditation programme which might serve as preparation for a larger prospective study. Semi-structured individual and group interviews with 54 students, 19 teachers and seven parents were carried out in three of these schools, each at the elementary level. Feedback from students, teachers and parents on the perceived effects of this programme indicated favourable impressions of programme benefits. Effects consistently cited included increased relaxation and feelings of calm, reduced stress, reduced anger and improved concentration. Many participants also reported that the experience of meditation at school had prompted them to meditate outside school, particularly at times of stress. A whole school approach appeared to facilitate more regular practice. This preliminary evaluation suggests that school-based meditation may represent an effective mental health promotion intervention worthy of further study. (Campion, 2009)

---

cation? As techniqued practices, they include MBSR (mindfulness-based stress reduction), MBCT (mindfulness-based cognitive therapy), DBT (dialectic behaviour therapy), ACT (acceptance and commitment therapy) (see Burke, 2010) and 'concentration methods' (*op cit*:135) such as TM (Transcendental Meditation). Also there are technique-less silence events such as pausing, staring out the window, going into a silent-space, dedicated quiet time and so on. It is therefore hard to develop a meaningful terminology that embraces all these practices. I broadly include them all in the phrase 'silence practices' and their study as 'silence studies'. People involved in these kinds of activities make use of silence in various ways. This is happening by deliberately introducing taught techniques or through other approaches. Schools are experimenting to find out what works for them in many locations.

Technique-less silence practices

The schools presented in chapters two and three show that the use of silence in schools is not in need of scientific research to show its benefits. Instead, an evolved and deeply understood system of beliefs and commitment to the idea of silence as beneficial proves to be rewarding

---

Schools using silence in assemblies

Kingswood School in Corby, Northamptonshire, sits in silence during assemblies for 'up to five minutes' (Naish, 2011). This practice was first instigated in 1965 by the school's first headteacher, Alan Bradley, a Quaker. In Quaker style the assembly was organised to reflect equality by arranging seating in a square. Commenting in a newspaper report, the current head-teacher, David Tristam, said: 'Sharing that amount of silence among so many people is very powerful, very special.' (*ibid*).

In **Sheringdale Primary**, south London, the new head teacher Kevin Hogston, who was previously at Latchmere School in Kingston upon Thames (see page 90) has introduced silence into assemblies (Paton, 2011) and wants to also investigate if choosing to pause briefly at the beginning and end of lessons can work for his classrooms.

---

to schools. The educational approaches are steeped in historical and long term experiences of using silence. These schools find cumulative experiences of silence with children and staff extending over months and years prove to have beneficial effects. The accounts described offer an overview of silence as a technology. They show that when nurtured, silence can create positive changes in school life – but they also speak of the challenge that silence presents in being a presence in a school.

A techniqued silence of meditation and mindfulness goes hand in hand with a holistic approach that incorporates simpler and shorter applications of silence such as pausing, standing still, gazing out the window (Lees, 2012), absenting oneself from a busy scene to a quieter place and so on. These simple activities can happen independent of the techniques of silence. In a school environment which has no other emphasis on integrating silence, they can be radical rebellions against busyness, bustle and noise. Personal in nature, technique-less silence actions are an anarchy of peace and calm against the culture of busyness in school.

Forms of technique-less silence are intriguing. These are the most important for education because no introductory teaching and learning is needed. They are a cost-free educational resource. No budget is required and they are available to all. Because they are so simple, accessible and obvious they bring benefits which are long term, not quick fixes.

Do silence practices require an ethics?

Some of the movements for silence practices do not take account of cumulative silence but are focused on interventions for improvement. The scale of introducing silence into schools and the implications for change and challenge to school systems are not always recognised.

The complex ethical terrain of silence in schools in terms of coercion, introduction, initiation, choice, options to not take part, to quit, to refuse, to abstain and so on is not yet fully understood. Conversations about how silence functions in education, how it ought to function and what other factors require debate are still ongoing. It cannot be taken for granted that silence in schools is a good thing. When seen as an 'intervention' silence is especially problematic because the factors of power that operate in schools confront the intimate and special nature of silence as an experience (Kalamaras, 1994; Orr, 2002).

Ethical stances are required towards the seemingly benign practice of silence because silence is powerful (see eg. Jaworski, 1993; Kenny, 2011). Silence needs to be talked about as though it could be a problem.

Thankfully, new voices are emerging which claim silence as a need and a right in schools (eg. Seldon, 2011; Thorpe, 2011). However, these authors speak frequently of the 'should' and the 'ought' of silence practices. A recent article strongly advocating 'stillness in schools' (Seldon, 2011), repeats the word 'should' seven times in a very short piece and also features 'must', 'responsibility', 'vital', 'not difficult', 'much easier'. Whilst I agree with the idea of silence in a school, I believe that silence that is introduced into a school by a headteacher or teacher with such sentiments: being easy, a responsibility and a matter of 'ought' misleads. Silence is neither easy nor is it an obligation. Once we appreciate how powerfully silence can affect the deepest self and the outcomes it can produce, it becomes clear that silence practices cannot be imposed on anyone as something they 'should' do.

A technology and curriculum of silence practices

Silence has a surprisingly intricate nature but when we work with it, we find a technology for managing it. Discovered over time, this technology is now filtering into modern practice. The scientific literature recognises how cumulative practice helps the efficacy of silence practices

84

in schools (Huppert and Johnson, 2010). It becomes evident that all matters 'silent' need care:

> Adapting MBSR/MBCT programs for younger participants requires attention to age-related developmental needs (attention span, cognitive capacities, language, physicality, relevant content), and issues arising from the fact that children are somewhat embedded within their family (and school) systems, and varyingly reliant on adults ... The embedded nature of children in family and school systems suggests the inclusion of caregivers and/or teachers, so they are informed, and able to support home (or school) practice, at the very least ... Other practical issues include the time involved in the interventions and home practice, competing with time demands of busy classrooms and family lives ... as well as ethical issues, including ensuring informed consent from both children and caregivers. (Burke, 2010:142-143)

Burke highlights the 'cautious 'small steps' approach needed in the early stages of research into a novel intervention' (*op cit*:139). Not all 'interventionists', however, adopt this approach.

Philanthropically motivated people are promoting meditation and silence for schools and children. They believe that meditative practices are good for people and especially for 'broken' children, and claim this is backed up by research – although the research is still in its infancy. Diverse and growing businesses are involved in silence practice activities. The media makes much of the enjoyment of the supposed newness of meditation and mindfulness, as saviours of these 'broken' children (see Hawn, 2011; Brand, 2011; Skidelsky, 2011). Many media articles recently have been discussing silence in all its forms: as noise antidote, health benefit, escape place, and so on. Debate about its place in society and how it is used is hitting the mainstream (see for example Sasso and Cecla, 2010; Codacci Pisanelli, 2010; Parks, 2010b; Rogers, 2011b; Naish, 2009; Mochi, 2010). Activity for 'modern' silence is an international affair, emerging for instance in Fiji (eg. McMahon and Mahony, 2011). Literature looking at silence from a number of philosophical and practical angles abounds in Europe (Fonteneau, 1999; Breton and Breton, 2009; de Smedt, 1986; Go, 2008; Andrieu, 2003; Jullien, 2009). Interest in silence is growing around the world.

Just to be deeply silent – even for a moment – involves giving up talk, money, results, progress and other aspects of a busy world. Silence as an experience is a world away from 'growth' and our usual thinking-for-achievement. Thinking how great a growth of silence could be for schools is to miss the point of silence. Silence practices might be best placed outside the curriculum and institutional improvement (eg. Rose, 2009; Tomlinson, 2004). They can be more in tune with post-modern attitudes to curriculum represented through, for instance, complexity theory where emergence is a key concept (eg. Doll, 1993; Osberg *et al*, 2008). How and why silence practices might enter the school curriculum will be interesting to watch. A technology of silence as 'other' than a current grammar of schooling (Tyack and Cuban, 1995) and a growth in its practices in schools means a new territory for educational studies is developing, since, for example: '... there is currently no curriculum for mindfulness or any clearly articulated objectives for mindfulness in schools ...' (Burnett, 2009:25).

Silence is golden

Reports of negative outcomes from silence practices are hard to find: 'no studies report any adverse affects' (Burke, 2010:136). Nataraja suggests that people with 'higher levels of psychological distress respond less well to regular meditative practice' (Nataraja, 2008:179) and this possibly raises questions about blanket introduction of silence practices into schools. But the ability for silence to be mentally dangerous applies to extreme situations such as solitary confinement, or the soundproofed anechoic chamber at Harvard said to be disturbingly silent for some people, among them the violinist who 'hammered on the door after a few seconds, demanding to be let out' (Foy, 2012). Such situations do not occur in schools.

Danger, then, is not an issue. Catching children young and exposing them to the soothing qualities of being silent could help them deal with any psychological distress – all children experience difficulties – and help them as they enter their adult lives. Journeying with silence is unique to each individual and each setting. A broad brush common sense assessment (see Erricker and Erricker, 2001) of whether silence practices in schools might fit with a number of government type agendas such as 'Every Child Matters' and 'Social, Emotional Aspects of Learning' suggests that silence in schools has potential (Weare, 2010). But we do have a responsibility in light of the significant affect silence practices can have.

Hollywood loves silence in schools

Endorsement by celebrities is increasing the profile of silence in schools. Hollywood stars such as Richard Gere, a Buddhist who started to meditate at the age of 24, helped to spread the idea in the 1990s that meditation was 'cool'. In 2005, movie director David Lynch set up his Foundation for Consciousness-Based Education and World Peace:

> ... to provide funding for stress-reducing, creativity-enhancing Transcendental Meditation programmes in state and private schools throughout the US and around the world. Since its launch over two years ago, the Foundation has raised more than $5 million and tens of thousands of students have learned to meditate as a result. (David Lynch Foundation, 2007)

Goldie Hawn also advocates silence practices in education. She has, it is alleged, met with Michael Gove, Secretary of State for Education to discuss setting up schools based on meditative principles relating to mindfulness practice and a curriculum that she calls 'MindUp™' in the UK (Skidelsky, 2011; *Daily Mail* Reporter, 2010) – the trade-mark speaks of business. The Hawn Foundation website states: 'With the support of our partners, MindUP™ is currently being implemented in hundreds of schools throughout the US, Canada, and the United Kingdom' (2011).

English TV and film personality Russell Brand is backing meditation for 'at-risk kids', through the Lynch Foundation asking for money to help it 'happen' (Brand, 2011). Silence practices are being introduced into schools through celebrity endorsement and Britain is, according to Skidelsky (2011), in the midst of a 'meditation boom'. All this echoes the attention paid to transcendental meditation after the Beatles visited the Maharishi in India in the 1960s.

Mental health agendas

Other initiatives, courses, projects and campaigns, such as the Mental Health Foundation's 'Be mindful' campaign (2011), suggest a different kind of agenda. Various research and teaching initiatives connected to meditation and mindfulness are being conducted at the Universities of Bangor, Oxford, Cambridge and Aberdeen. There is much activity in the United States, such as at the Garrison institute and the Mind & Life Institute, as well as universities like UCLA and University of Massachusetts Medical School. Both have centres for mindfulness research (see appendix for weblinks). Some of this work is connected to education and some to health and well-being. The growing number of publications and resources that can be connected to silence practices for a popular market (eg. Hanson and Mendius, 2009, Begley, 2009, Doidge, 2007) are associated with the rise of neuroscience and its claims to improve mental function.

Mindfulness practices are being recommended for use on the National Health Service for the treatment of recurring depressive symptoms (National Institute for Health and Clinical Excellence, 2009) and 'clinical interventions based on training in mindfulness skills are described with increasing frequency and their popularity appears to be growing rapidly' (Baer, 2003:125).

Well resourced philanthropic bodies such as the Templeton Foundation are funding activities relating to 'meditation's practical power' to the tune of over a million dollars (John Templeton Foundation, 2010). In 2012 the Foundation awarded the Dalai Lama the Templeton Prize, in part to acknowledge his involvement in linking cognitive science and Buddhism's contemplative practices. This prize is to celebrate spiritual progress activities and in terms of prize money it tops the Nobel prize.

All this activity is significant for silence in schools, because it highlights its relevance and desirability.

Silence practice in specific schools

School education functions largely with discourse: '... mainstream contemporary educational systems ... emphasise language as the only way we know or learn about the world' (Zembylas and Michaelides, 2004: 209). However, some schools use silence in ways suited to their needs, purposes, ethos and philosophy. So the practices vary from school to school.

What all the schools featured tend to aim for in their use of silence is to foster calm, self-awareness and appreciation of others. Some explore the possible benefits of silence for academic achievement but the primary interest is for silence to be a transformer of consciousness, sense of self and interpersonal attitudes, and to influence how children see, and are in, the world. 'Silent schools' can be found around the world, although they are still a tiny percentage.

Neohumanist and Maharishi schools

Neohumanist schools around the world, including the independent co-ed **Sunrise Primary School** in North London, use yoga and meditation to create silence:

> Yoga and Meditation are practiced daily at the beginning of the day... Meditation helps to calm and concentrate the mind and still the body, freeing the mind from both internal and external distractions, as the children peacefully center themselves for the busy day ahead. (Neohumanist Education, 2009)

For the past 25 years, the independent co-ed **Maharishi School** in Lancashire has been practicing meditation twice daily for 5 to 20 minutes each time, depending on the age of the children. It is one of approximately 200 Maharishi inspired schools around the world using transcendental meditation. The school has children from primary through to year eleven. It describes itself as:

> [a] wonderful place to be – a dynamic learning environment combines with a harmonious atmosphere, in which children aged 4-16 receive the uniquely effective system of Consciousness Based Education (Maharishi School, 2011)

Recently this school was approved as a free school under the new regime of state funding introduced by the Coalition government. In the context of setting up further schools based on the Maharishi principles of silence, the headmaster of the Maharishi school, Derek Cassells, is reported as saying:

> I'm certain that transcendental meditation can work on a bigger scale... The key factor is that the meditation brings balance to the nervous system. This leads to greater creativity, intelligence and harmony, and better behaviour. (Marley, 2009)

Apart from the well known schools with a history of silence practices which have been established as part of their ethos or curriculum, it is not possible to determine the extent of such practices in schools at present. That practice is growing is clear from numerous new school names being mentioned in articles and anecdotally reported on. But who does what is not being captured as data; neither is the practice monitored. Meditation and mindfulness practices in schools occurs currently in the spirit of the comment by UK2 in chapter two:

St James Schools

The **St James Schools** are three schools in the London area, a primary school and a girls senior school in Olympia and a boys senior school in Twickenham. All practice pausing at the beginning and end of lessons. They have meditation in assemblies for the older children and, in the boy's school, two sessions per day of ten minutes of meditation. All children have the option to learn to meditate if they wish. This silence practice has been happening since 1975. (see appendix)

Examples of schools using meditation as a practice

For the past four years the co-ed state **Latchmere School** in Kingston upon Thames has offered one hour per week for each child to meditate in the school's sanctuary space 'The Blue Room'. The meditation practices have been so popular with the children that they have started a meditation club (Wilce, 2009).

In **Sacred Heart Primary School** in Loughborough, Sr. Anna Patricia Pereira has been working with children to introduce them to meditation, using a mantra. She reports that the children become leaders of the sessions, preparing for themselves a 'sacred space' by putting up notices around the room indicating time for silence, laying out special meditation mats and following a sequence of music, chimes and mantra recitation, all done with reverence for the ritual. The children have, she writes, gained a liking for meditation and 'have requested to have a session before their SATS exam' among other times. (Pereira, 2011)

> I heard of a school today, somebody said to me that they've started meditation with children in year seven or something ... not with the rest of the school, but they'd started practising meditation with year seven.

Hollywood endeavours are new activity for silence in schools, but UK groups with a philosophical or religious orientation are also organising themselves to instigate wide access to techniqued practices. Following a seminar in London in 2010 on Meditation and Education, it was reported that a new Working Group of the National Community of Christian Meditation was active:

... currently they are working with 97 UK schools (primary and secondary) that are implementing meditation programs with the students in the classroom, and they continue to receive new requests from other schools. (Wulff, 2011)

Silence practices as a commitment

There is much research presenting evidence of the health and social benefits of silence practice such as meditation (see the weblinks appendix for more information.) When it comes to school settings, the research field is still emerging, but it already explores some interesting themes. On the role of regular practice, for instance, Linden asks whether inconsistencies in the results of his 1973 research might be due to an absence of regularity and factors of time spent involved in practice:

> An alternative explanation is that meditation is a skill that requires practice over a long period of time, and only after a certain level of adeptness has been attained, fairly consistently, do the effects of the practice ramify. (Linden, 1973:142)

In a 2010 study, Huppert asks the same question:

> Our finding that *amount of practice* was significantly related to improvements on two of the three outcome measures (mindfulness and well-being), despite students having had less than 3 hours of mindfulness training (compared with typically 16 hours for adults), suggests that this is a very promising intervention for adolescents. (Huppert and Johnson, 2010:270 emphasis added)

Any regular, long term meditator is likely to say that regular practice is important. As the UK5 practitioner highlighted in chapter three describes, practising with silence in the form of various techniques is not necessarily about peace and calm:

> ... we've been talking a lot about calm and quiet and stillness of the mind. Mindfulness is not just about that. That is an aspect of it. But mindfulness is also about dealing with the mind when it's choppy and observing the mind when it's difficult, which might even make it worse for a period of time. And [once] learnt, placing mindfulness in the context of stress, anxiety, anger is critical.

Maintaining practice regularly helps to obtain a long-term overview of its effects. A consistent account of good days and bad days offers an amalgamated, levelled perspective of life's ups and downs which is more useful than the emotions of the moment. With experience, meditators can understand that there may be periods when silence practices are unsatisfying, but they can take the long view.

For children, one minute of silent practice for each year of age is often used as appropriate. If they find it unsatisfactory, children are unlikely to be disheartened when it is soon over. Brief meditative experiences give school children a taste of mature meditation demanding dedica-tion, regular unbroken practice, information, personal research and trial and error. Also needed often are the right clothing, the right sitting position, the right way of regularity, the right timings in the day and so on (see Kabat-Zinn, 2011, for a guide to some techniques and condi-tions) but this is unrealistic and unnecessary in school settings.

Mindfulness and meditation in schools is best seen as an *introduction* to an activity that the children can embark on at school for life-long personal learning and exploration. Schools cannot offer a serious pro-gramme of in-depth silence within the span of school attendance. It cannot be said to be *taught* in a school, like history or maths. It is, as UK5 says, 'caught', not programmed.

Although the duration of children's meditation should not be too long, the research about silence practices in the domains of adult health (eg. Davidson *et al*, 2003), children's health (eg. Barnes *et al*, 2004), adult well-being (eg. Pruett *et al*, 2007) and children's well-being (eg. Harrison *et al*, 2004) does have implications for any level of practice. Even the lightest long term or even certain short term practice (say, an eight week course) seems to have effects. Studies of meditation in schools that use scientific methods such as control groups are conducted over mere weeks and certainly less than a year. Yet they report similar findings to those of Linden in that:

> The results confirm that children can be taught this discipline and apparently with beneficial results ... the results encourage further investigation of medi-tation as a training method of self-discovery and self-mastery. (Linden, 1973: 142)

Similarly, Huppert and Johnson report '... significant findings ... using only a short intervention' (2010:272). Levete notes the wider benefits that discrete meditation practice seems to facilitate:

The purpose of meditation practice is to benefit not only the period of quiet sitting but also to benefit the rest of the day ... Verbal feedback from students who have been introduced to different methods of meditation at school indicates that this can be so. As part of an enquiry into meditation in schools, students of different ages and different backgrounds were invited to express their views about meditation. Some students attended state schools, others independent ones. Their overall perspectives were remarkably similar. Most of them preferred to regard meditation as a spiritual practice, 'though not religious', which also was of therapeutic and practical benefit. (Levete, 2001d: 10)

Non-techniqued silence practices

Meditation and mindfulness are key techniqued silence practices in schools, but there are others. Levete suggests that no one can advocate an ideal method and that each 'in its own way produces a positive effect' (Levete, 2001a:22). She identifies a number of different meditative techniques that could be used, such as 'connecting to the body', walking meditation, mantra meditation, visualisation, mind observation and following the breath (*ibid*). Two which she does not mention, which both have no taught technique, are of particular importance: pausing and silent spaces.

These technique-less silences belong to the state of mind I call strong silence, functioning as building blocks and aids towards it. The effect of pausing in schools is of particular interest, and warrants research. Like silent spaces, pausing fosters a whole school ethos of silence and can play a role in the democratisation of schools discussed in the next chapter.

Silent pauses in schools

In *Silence, the Phenomenon and its Ontological Significance*, Bernard Dauenhauer identifies different types of silence (1980), one set of which is made up of 'intervening' silence and 'fore-and-after silence', or pauses. One of the uses of pauses is to create a 'closing-opening operation' that can both 'melodically' and 'rhythmically" punctuate events involving speech 'utterances' (*op cit*:6). It is 'the aspect of silence which is involved in timing and pacing' (*op cit*:7). According to Dauenhauer:

> These occurrences of silence are just as essential to the rhythm of the totality as are any of the sound phrases which make up the utterance. The appropriate number, placement, and duration of intervening silences are just as

important to the dramatic, if not to the lexical, sense of a story as the appropriately proportioned length, internal balance, etc, of the sound phrases. This fact is especially evident when one considers a piece of music. But it holds good for discourse of all sorts. (*ibid*)

Most classroom teaching is paced so the lesson can be managed. But at micro level, the profession of teaching seems not to take account of the

Wait time

Research by Rowe suggested that proper prolonged pausing as a teaching art was almost unheard of: only three out of 200 teachers in a science classroom took their time and allowed students to answer within a 'wait time', as she called a pause:

> With the exception of a few teachers (three in 200 recordings), the pace of instruction was very fast. Teachers allowed students an average time of only 1 sec to start an answer to a question. If a response did not commence within 1 sec, teachers usually either repeated the question or called on others to respond. When students did respond, teachers usually waited slightly less than a second (average of 0.9 sec) before commenting on the response (reacting), asking another question (soliciting), or moving to a new topic (structuring). (Rowe, 1974:207)

The effect of this was to lessen the quality of the instruction. Rowe identified that wait time of three seconds or more was required for students to respond. When the study was expanded beyond the initial curriculum science initiative, teachers were almost all unable to wait for more than three seconds and interrupted silence within a three second span. When a wait-time pause was made by the teacher, students' response length increased, whereas 'under a fast schedule, responses tend to consist of short phrases and rarely exhibit explanation of any complexity' (*ibid*:217). Under a slow-time schedule, there were fewer failures to respond, the confidence of the students' responses rose and they made more unsolicited appropriate responses, showed greater complexity of thinking and experimental ideas, asked more questions, and the slower-in-response students contributed more. Overall, Rowe found that 'changes in wait time shift the game towards a more equitable state' (*op cit*:207). Greater interaction was one effect but there was also greater inclusion: 'Unsolicited comments from teachers over the last five years on longer wait-time schedules indicate that members of the bottom group perform in new and surprising ways' (*op cit*:221).

internal rhythm of the discourse of teaching and learning. Pausing properly, as a deliberate and discrete stillness, is seldom recognised as part of the art of teaching. In the St James Schools (see page 90 and appendix), pausing is an integral part of the school day, because their pedagogic philosophy is influenced in this specific regard by the Russian mystic Serge Gurdjieff. During the first half of the 19th century, he taught his followers a system of living that focused on being present in the moment. Integrated into this approach was pausing (Gurdjieff, 1984 edition).

Only these schools are influenced by Gurdjieff, but pausing can work, educationally and mentally, to encourage a state of mind that is open to slow reflection and making sense of things.

Most schools have not come to value pauses and their quality as spaces empty of discourse with no information, no questions, no interaction.

Information overload: the need for breaks

Research is showing that information overload in a technological age and the fast speed of its delivery is actually causing the brain to 'freeze'. The following is an extract from a *Newsweek* article, 'I Can't Think!'

> The booming science of decision making has shown that more information can lead to objectively poorer choices, and to choices that people come to regret. It has shown that an unconscious system guides many of our decisions, and that it can be sidelined by too much information. And it has shown that decisions requiring creativity benefit from letting the problem incubate below the level of awareness – something that becomes ever-more difficult when information never stops arriving ... Creative decisions are more likely to bubble up from a brain that applies unconscious thought to a problem, rather than going at it in a full-frontal, analytical assault. So while we're likely to think creative thoughts in the shower, it's much harder if we're under a virtual deluge of data. 'If you let things come at you all the time, you can't use additional information to make a creative leap or a wise judgment,' says Cantor. 'You need to pull back from the constant influx and take a break.' That allows the brain to subconsciously integrate new information with existing knowledge and thereby make novel connections and see hidden patterns. (Begley, 2011)

Today's children are surrounded by constant input and interaction and many schools are not helping them to deal with this in applied ways. Theoretical research on a right for children to stare blankly out the classroom window as a form of down-time and escape, and schools allowing such reflective freedoms, suggests there is much scope for new attitudes to the school as mental and communal space (Lees, 2012).

Thus there is a need to deliberately pause in schools if staff are not already aware of such mental breaks. But can schools benefit from integrated pauses?

> Are we able and willing to consider the practical value of silence for a child who simply needs time to think? Or is the potential for 'wasted time' likely to stop the teacher from exploring with her students the meaning, value, self-discipline and trust that is a necessary prerequisite for the freedom to create and refine ideas. (Haskins, 2010:5)

Li criticises Rowe's wait-time for its instrumental aspect. Just because pausing helps learning does not mean it is necessarily being used as a silent mode. She argues:

> In line with Rowe's study, many teachers learn to utilise silent wait-time in the process of teaching. To a large extent, they may be aware that a moment of silent wait-time is an essential temporal space for thinking and reflection. However, the current accountability movement is so outcome driven that many teachers are inclined to view silence as a mechanic device for soliciting observable and measurable responses. In other words, silence as a pedagogical action may not be grounded in teachers' mindful reflections on teaching and learning. (Huey-li, 2001:160)

So pausing as beneficial, special and new in school education has to be part of a philosophy of education that is not means-end oriented. For pausing in the classroom to have educational meaning requires a pause in the thinking going on.

Pausing schools

The headteachers in chapter 2 talk about pauses in their schools. They have established an art of using a considered pause that carries more weight than just waiting a bit. They use it regularly at the start and end of discrete activities such as assembly, a staff meeting, in lessons. UK1 described use of pausing (see pages 13 and 25) which it is useful to repeat here:

HL: 'You say let's have a pause. How do they react when you say that?'

UK1: 'Well, they just do it. I just say *listen* and as soon as you say it there's this amazing space. They don't just stand there being odd. You just say it and they listen ... It's unusual to have a school that's pausing and having access to this quiet but it is absolutely normal. I don't see it as something quirky and nor do the staff ... It's a kind of fresh start and then a close of it ... English doesn't run into maths ... It's very unifying because everybody is doing it.

HL: Does it make your life easier?

UK1: Yes it does! There's a start to something and an end to something and a time to reflect and it can provide inspiration for a lesson ... I don't know how teachers manage without it. It's just a way of gathering together everyone's attention ... it almost harnesses potential ...

Here we can see ideas of allowing the mind to relax, the body to regain a regular breathing rhythm and for awareness of oneself in the moment. This echoes what thinkers such as Thich Nhat Hanh say about becoming aware through focus on the breath:

> Through awareness of breathing, we can be awake in (and to) the present moment. By being attentive, we have already established 'stopping,' i.e. concentration of mind. (Nhat Hanh, 1990:44)

Educationally, this possibility is identified by Haskins as going against most current school practice:

> It goes without saying that as long as our educational system remains standards-based and maintains a structure in which all students study the same thing at the same time, there will be little room for practices that support pause, pondering, or for breath-based exercises. (Haskins, 2010)

I disagree – even if the system is standards-based and structured, it is still made up of people. All it takes in education for the basics of pausing to infiltrate is for people to resist by stopping. Simply stopping. And what is to prevent them? To briefly do nothing and to see what comes out of that might be a radical move. Yet this alone could possibly change the nature of the education system. The impact of a few seconds of silence is possibly the starting point for fundamental school change. But were this practice to gain currency, the change can only begin when teachers feel comfortable with silence and do not feel they need to fill it with their own voice:

Two participants commented on how often teachers intruded on that type of positive communal silence by comments like 'Isn't everyone being quiet?', by doing so actually subverting the silence. (Ollin, 2008)

Writing this book has brought me to an amazing conclusion: at the heart of silence in schools and at the heart of a change in education is pausing. Everything else this book discusses emerges from this possibility of a small beginning.

To emphasise the point I will

pause.

At a deep level, pausing is part of a way of thinking that is contrary to western ideas. Within the deep complexity of the eastern Zen tradition, Masters help their disciples stop thinking in habitual limited ways that are flawed by these limits. They use koans: paradoxical sentences with no logical sense. The paradox inhabits and inhibits the mind from following its normal reasoning paths. It is the pausing of the mind which koans effect that gives the Zen disciple a way to stop moving forward inexorably in a fixed, already known direction of thought. The disruption of the usual neural pathways causes otherwise thinking: a pause in the normal and normalising. In this deeper sense of pausing, a solid, communally agreed pause in a school day is a space of freedom for thinking to not be directed.

Levete suggests that pauses can also be 'an effective way of preparing very young students for meditation at a later time' (2001b:70).

Koans as pausing

Koans are paradoxical sayings, used in Zen practice as a teaching method for thinking differently: to stop the mind from processing thought in its usual way and offer a possible enlightenment event, where things fall into place with a new perspective for sense-making (see Reps, 2000). Walls discusses briefly using koans with a group of students in the context of doing Tai Chi exercises for silent effects of calm and collected self (Wall, 2005). Koans indicate an interesting silence practice for future use with children and an area for research.

Silence for one minute or one day only
'Day of Silence 2009'; 'The Big Hush 2008'; or timed remembrance of tragic events such as WWI or 9/11 inspire occasional minutes or sponsored days of silence in schools, to support anti-harassment campaigns. This is not the silence I am discussing, although it might serve as a momentary introduction to it. In the USA, however, successful legislative fights in six states for the holding of secular silent minutes at the beginning of the school day could be considered in line with the idea of strong silence because of their *regularity* as part of the community life of the school (Masters, 2001).

However, silent pausing in schools has been seen as a problem. In several states in America, the matter of a daily one minute silent pause has been taken to the courts. The idea of moments of deliberate silence in a school at the start of the day is interpreted by some state jurisdictions to be unconstitutional, as crossing 'the line separating church and state'; hiding prayer under a pretext, a 'thinly disguised effort to bring religion into schools' (Fox News, 2009). Such issues are clearly not applicable in a UK context where some form of daily worship is expected of schools.

To say that silence is in some way religious is as valid as to say it is secular. The pausing discussed here as beneficial for school settings may indeed be partly spiritual but this book looks at the benefits to mental health and thinking style, and the rhythmic aspects to do with change from constant rush and busyness. The idea of pausing in schools is

---

Technique-less stillness in lessons
Quaker schools around the UK and Ireland, the **St James Schools** in London, and the **Krishnamurti Brockwood Park School** in Hampshire all use pausing at the start and end of activities as they feel appropriate. Other schools are now beginning to understand the scholastic and personal benefits of this practice. The independent school **Wellington College**, near Reading, has begun to include weekly '15 minute slots of stillness' for 13-15 year olds in its wellbeing classes. (Seldon, 2011). The headmaster considers it is 'a school of today in the work that we do on stillness...' (Seldon, 2010).

---

linked more to movements for slow food and slow living (see Petrina and Padovani, 2005; Parkins and Craig, 2006) than it is to prayer. But prayer too is a pause in unreflective being and becoming, so the type of pause discussed here has much in common with prayer. Arguably, pausing of this 'slow' kind ought to be more regular during a school day than just the once in the morning that provoked controversy in the US.

Silent spaces in schools

There is something magical about having a place to retreat to; a sanctuary for the mind that is laden with thoughts.

> I believe that children, when they have a chance, naturally seek out places of quiet to be alone with their own thoughts – a tree house, a little hut, an attic room or a secluded garden. Many people's biographies include descriptions of special places where, as children, they could wallow in privacy and let their imagination run free. (Wolf, 2007:12)

Silent spaces are normal for children because they find them helpful. They make them, they hunt for them. What schools can do is facilitate and meet this need. The need for silent spaces in the midst of a hectic school day is not only for children, though – it is also for staff.

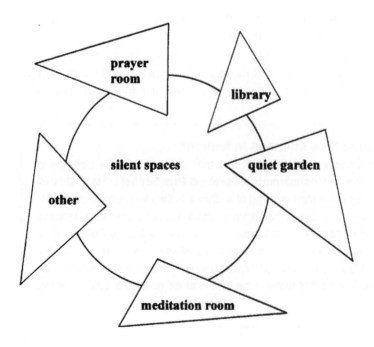

Given the intense pace of the school day, with shouted instructions, ringing bells, movement between activities, lessons, objectives, venues, multiple social interaction, it is no wonder that people in schools might want time out in silence. It is more surprising that not all schools appreciate this human need. John Lane criticises state education for this ignorance:

> ... the State's educational system has not been designed for personal development; it has been designed to discourage any serious semblance of critical thought ... it is important to remember the value of thinking for oneself, which is best done in silence. (Lane, 2006:57-58)

Silence might involve a space away from the talk of others; accessed whenever needed. Some schools and teachers have always been aware of children's inclination and need to escape to a quiet, private place. When staff have felt a similar need to be alone, still, quiet or reflective they seek a special place away from it all – as teachers tell me they have done, and as I did when I worked in a school. I would wander around the edges of the grassed area at the back of the school, looking for a silent nook behind an outbuilding, often to find children had got there first. Eventually I settled, as had the one Muslim child for his prayers, for

---

Quiet spaces in schools

Bilton School in Rugby has a peace garden 'where they can go to sit quietly' (Staff Writer, 2009). **Norton Primary School** in Stockton on Tees gives children 'a place to sit in peace away from the main playground' as part of its 'Eco-Schools' project. (Eco Schools, 2011). **The Anglo European School** in Essex has been trying for some years to raise sufficient funds to turn a disused outbuilding into a space for silence and reflection, similar to the Dag Hammarskjöld space the United Nations has in its New York headquarters. The fundraising campaign says: 'imagine a quiet place in a busy school...' and the building is gradually progressing (Anglo European School, 2012). **Ruskin Junior School** in Swindon is one school amongst others in the area that has turned a disused classroom into a 'tranquillity room'. The school reports that this facility is 'improving exam results and boosting children's self esteem' as well as helping some children sleep better. It is said to have inspired some of the parents to set up similar tranquillity spaces at home (Maddern, 2011).

a windowless meeting room facing onto a busy corridor. There was nowhere else to go – although the school has since created a sanctuary space. But few schools seem to understand a dedicated place to be still, quiet and silent that – apart from a need for prayer facilities – is an educational facility for children and staff, if the whole school is an educational environment.

Research cited in this book presents evidence that constant noise and stimulation is counter-productive for educational ends and people's general well-being. But standard provision policy for silent places to retreat to in schools is so far lacking in educational thinking. There is little recognition that schools should function slowly, calmly and with respect for personal inner reflection.

Montessori education is well aware of children's need for silence experiences and has developed learning exercises about silence and respect for its place in the school setting:

> One hundred years ago, when the environment was much less noisy than it is today, Maria Montessori saw the need to give children regular experiences of silence. To do this she devised The Silence Game, a group exercise that presented silence, not as a punishment, but as a special challenge – something to be achieved. (Wolf, 2007:13)

The silence game

The 'Lesson in silence' was a game Maria Montessori played with the children in her school and which Montessori teachers still use. It involves showing small children something silent (Montessori's own written example is of a small baby asleep) and asking the children to learn from this silent thing how to be silent; stimulating them to think about what silence is as absence of speaking and movement. Montessori suggested to the children that none of them could be as silent as the little child and this made them try their hardest to be silence personified by not moving or making a sound (Montessori, 1990).

Another way in which Montessori taught the children about silence was to 'stand or sit silent and motionless...I call a child and invite him to act as I do ...the children remain fascinated as they look and listen. Very many become interested in a fact which they have never before observed...that there are different degrees of silence'. (*op cit*.140)

Montessori deliberately included silent spaces in her schools, as here:

> Some teachers who are attuned to the value of silence create a Quiet Corner where one child at a time can enjoy several minutes away from the class-room activity. Here a child can observe a fish tank or sit at a little table and examine a beautiful seashell, arrange a group of unusual stories or simply look out the window at nature. (Wolf, 2007:13)

In a beautiful story told by Haskins about a young boy, the healing power of a silent space for someone with emotional trauma (see Picard, 2002; Sardello, 2008; Le Clair, 2009; Parks, 2010a) is depicted:

> ... I made a quiet area directly outside the classroom door, where a large window provided a view of the pastoral country setting beyond. On the wall I hung a peaceful poster of a young child on the grass holding a small bunny, and on a small wooden TV table I placed my homemade rock garden. I brought out a wicker chest donated by a parent, upon which I placed a large, thriving philodendron plant. It was a simple setting, but James, a tense, hesitant, distrusting child, was clearly drawn to it; he used it often, along with the other children. I saw how raking the paths around the pebbles in the rock garden calmed him. Sometimes he just sat and looked out the window. At the end of the year he gave me a hand drawn picture of himself in the classroom and across the top he had written, *I love this class. I wish I could be in it next year.* From then on, I always found a way to incorporate a quiet/peace area in my classroom. (Haskins, 2010:5)

Conclusion

This chapter offers an overview of silent practices in schools, but it is only a snapshot of what is going on. In the latter section, I have focused on pausing and silent spaces, as I think these practices are being over-looked in the enthusiasm for mindfulness and meditation.

That schooling does not offer any of these practices as standard seems a wasted opportunity for enhancing the educational environment. The resource of silence – especially when technique-less – is low cost or cost-free, yet it is still not part of policy.

Perhaps schools are failing to look towards silence practices because the concept of silence and its use in education is still new to many. These days media exposure is required for anything to take off. Now that people are promoting silence practices via TED lectures, Youtube, email newsletters, seminars, events, conferences and other avenues, silence in schools is acquiring a profile.

I have tried to sound a note of caution. Silence in schools needs to be deeply considered and not used only for its proven benefits. Education is often too quick to grasp a new technique and force it onto students and staff and this could be counter-productive with silence, as it challenges current school environments. Research is needed about its community impact as a radical intervention so that practitioners can think in an informed way about taking up silence practices.

Silence demands time to bear its positive fruit, so we need to ask certain questions. For instance, how is silence going to function in a school that has no philosophical underpinning for silence practice? Most of the schools mentioned in this chapter do have a philosophical background and foundation.

There may come a day when scientific and qualitative evidence suggests that silence is an educational 'must-have' and policy makers advise that it should have a place in every school. The base would be the research and debate that is now going on and which needs to go further. Practices will work to best advantage if the school understands how silence fits into education. For this, school staff, students, parents, researchers and those with policy power need to discuss together what they believe silence in schools is and can be.

6
The power of silence
in schools

Introduction

Silence is identified by Dauenhauer (1980) and Picard (2002), among others, as a positive phenomenon which exists independently from speech or music; it is a force and power with a life of its own. Kenny (2011) and Jaworski (1993) associate silence with power. Both chose 'The Power of Silence' as the title for their respective overviews of silence, in which they discuss its breadth, depth, impact and reach from various perspectives. Like others (eg. Maitland, 2008; Sim, 2007; Clair, 1998; Tannen and Saville-Troike, 1995; Kurzon, 1998; Picard, 2002), they see silence as important. I have identified three specific forms of this power that belong to education, especially in schools.

- Silence has the power to release schools from pre-structured, cognitive, rational orientations of thinking and enable a shift towards more fluid, emergent and creative modes. Thinking-through-silence does not operate through binaries and dualism so it allows freedom from the ingrained oppositions of right and wrong which permeate everything from behaviour to exam results and enforce a testing-assessment mentality.

- Silence has the power to bring democratic experiences into schools. As we saw in chapter four, most schools are not democratically inclined; they operate through structures of authority and hierarchy. These can cause abuses of power which have a negative impact on children and staff. How the introduction of silence can increase democracy in all schools is discussed below.

■ Silence has the ability to undo externalisation of the self. Children are in thrall to the internet, playstations, magazines and television telling them how to look and behave, even think. Silence has the power to return people to themselves and be independent of the matrixed, binary 'code' of the world (Baudrillard and Guillaume, 2008). It provides spaces for escape from being locked into a code of expectations, assumptions, demands and can thus make schooling a personal journey. Education can be about what is unique in an individual and which can emerge from that uniqueness (Biesta, 2006). Silence offers a way back from homogenising forces and commercial concerns (Hartley, 2008) to the genuinely personal, devoid of a means-end mentality.

These three powers of silence are connected. A way of thinking that refuses to think that a person is right or wrong is linked to a more democratic way for education in schools to develop: dialogue, and not authority, determines what is right or wrong. Thus the power of silence in schools to facilitate epistemologies and mechanisms of thinking that are non-binary and non-conceptual and which highlight the inner self rather than promoting externalisation, creates an anti-oppressive way of education that is inherently democratic. Subservience to authority via codes of morality which see things in black and white is exposed. Attitudes are changed by silence. As Orr (2002) avers:

> Of particular importance for antioppressive teachers is the insight ... that people reify binaristically constructed concepts of self, gender, race, and a host of other categories with which they then identify and to which they become deeply attached at the same time that they assign the oppositional terms to others. (Orr, 2002:491)

I am assuming that democracy is desirable in schools, that thinking outside the box and personal creativity is wanted; that being true to oneself is helpful. We need young people to take an active, informed part in society and to have a personal understanding of what it means to be part of a democracy (eg. Crick, 1998; Lawy *et al*, 2009). We need young people who are problem solvers and do not unquestioningly accept authority or believe that how things are is the only way they can be. We need them to challenge the status quo through thoughtful dialogue if it seems unfair or wrong and to build the world imaginatively, using resources that do not strip the planet (eg. Arendt, 2006; Wilkinson and Pickett, 2009; Princen, 2010). Taking care of oneself makes it possible to think of others (Foucault, 1986). Silence creates a space for thinking about such matters and about taking care of oneself and of others, which is important in democratic societies. But schools are failing to prepare children adequately to meet the exigencies of a democratically functioning world. A way out of democratic deficiency in the school system might be found in an appreciation of the power of silence.

The power of silence to think otherwise

Kenny suggests that 'To be or to fall silent is a way of enhancing other ways of being ...' (2011:px). Dauenhauer points out that silence is a means by which the intentional can be circumvented or remain untouched (1980:82). These ideas are echoed in new theories of 'obliquity' – that doing things indirectly achieves more (Kay, 2011). Silence is able to lay open situations and circumstances to unintentionality and to free people from having a defined object to their discourse, intentions and actions. Silence is the platform upon which new things can happen, discoveries can be made, people can re-imagine. Potential is released from the silence that can be translated into discourse and action.

How silence affects teaching style and strategy for classroom management is illustrated by maths teacher Alf, as he sets out to create an engaging lesson:

> Alf was aware that his silence had forced students to think for themselves about what he was doing, putting the onus of explanation on them. (Brown and Coles, 2008:32)

> Into an energised space Alf said, 'What's different about what you've been doing with Miss Brown and what we were doing last lesson?' The effect of this question was to make the group absolutely still. This was a silence in the students that was of a different quality to that experienced before – a stillness. (From lesson observation notes)

> The silence energy which we had identified ... was energetic and mobilising for the learners, their attention was focused in the present and they were using themselves in the moment bringing everything they have with them to restructure their experience. ... stillness seemed to be trapped by the invitation to compare two aspects of experience, before and after, and it was as if the students' present attention looked inward to attend to that difference. This stillness was also a powerful silence but not about experience, more about synthesis. There had been the question and this was the reaction – this stillness was their will, not imposed by the teacher. (*op cit*:34)

What we see is the students thinking, emerging into new states and releasing energy, all allowed by silence. It does not involve a machinery of thought such as a lesson plan. As UK1 said about a silent pause in chapter two: 'It kind of brings it to a point you don't know where it's going to go to and that's exciting teaching ...' (see page 25).

According to Tobin Hart (2004), most school teaching has a relationship to knowledge characterised by 'the dominance of a largely Aristotelian logic, the natural sciences, and theology beginning at least by the 12th and 13th centuries and consolidated in the reformation or scientific revolution ...' (Hart, 2004:29). This emphasis on a way of thinking that is '... linear, analytical, and product-oriented ...' (*op cit*:34) is, Hart suggests, a narrow vision. Kalamaras (1994) too maintains that many forms of institutional education are limited by a binary-oriented conceptual approach, informed only by the western philosophical canon. Kalamaras sees this framework for thought and knowledge as the reason why those in the west tend to automatically cast silence 'as a negative condition', which he considers is 'largely erroneous' (*op cit*:3).

The strangulation of education because of binary thinking, stuck in a framework of opposites of right and wrong, good and bad, appropriate and inappropriate, has been identified as a limitation by teachers themselves:

> An early realisation was ... I did not want to be needed by the students to tell them if what they were doing was right/wrong or to tell them what they had to do next. I was most comfortable if the students had a question or problem which they were discussing amongst themselves, trying to convince each other about what was the case, without the need for me to authorise or validate their thinking. (Brown and Coles, 2008:13-14)

Thinkers such as Fritjof Capra (1990), Seymour Papert (1993), Giles Deleuze and Félix Guattari (2004) and Michel Foucault (1977) argue that systems of thought can codify and ossify until they seem to be the only way. In the words of Deleuze and Guattari:

> We're tired of trees. We should stop believing in trees, roots, and radicles. They've made us suffer too much. All of arborescent culture is founded on them, from biology to linguistics. Nothing is beautiful or loving or political aside from underground stems and aerial root, adventitious growths and rhizomes. (Deleuze and Guattari, 2004:15)

Staying locked in the known and the mapped can be destructive and counter-productive. Writers on education and silence argue that alternative, contemplative ways of thinking, which silence has the power to facilitate, can reshape education. Such thinking does not follow train tracks, map routes or 'roots and radicles', because silence does not use the binaries and dualities of language and has no 'DNA as an ordering determinant' (Baudrillard, 1993). Contemplative styles of thought such as reflection, waiting, pondering, wondering have 'cognitive gaps that allow for the possibility of conceptual flexibility and multiplicity' (Hart, 2004:34). There is an absence of foreclosures and this:

> ... invites an inner opening of awareness. This opening within us in turn enables a corresponding opening toward the world before us. Through a fresh lens, our worldview, sense of self and the relationships may be powerfully transformed (*op cit*:29).

Hart goes on:

> What we know about education is that one shoe does not fit all; students' varying learning styles, interests and capacities require variation in teaching. The same may be true in contemplation. Different paths may work better for different people (*op cit*:34).

Berryman discusses this in the context of the imaginative powers that silence nurtures. If imagination is not harnessed, life in every sphere is impoverished:

> In this postmodern age of words about words, it is a matter of ethical importance to slow down, to listen until we hear, and to respect the silence in other people, in our own deep self, in nature, and in God. The ethics of the imagination is a matter of respect for 'the other', but it is also an ethic of emergency. The ability to hear silence may be dying out. If that happens, then

the imagination will disintegrate. It is true that what humans do with our imagination often endangers the world, but without it we lack even the possibility of coping with destructive tendencies. (Berryman, 1999:267)

Importantly, the contemplative attitude cannot be coerced or cajoled into action just because a schooling system has recognised its usefulness. A form of structured thinking, productive and goal-oriented, would be seeking to act upon a way of thinking that is essentially formless. A contemplative way of thinking has no connection with assumptions of structure. It is not through force that the mood or state of mind of the contemplative self comes into being but through spontaneous, free emergence. 'The contemplative mind cannot be willed, as it arises spontaneously, but it can be welcomed' (Hart, 2004:34).

Silence provides a structure-less background for spontaneity of mind and self to arise. UK2 spoke about 'a bed of silence' in the school (see page 21). For schools to introduce contemplative aspects that emerge from awareness of silence, the tools of current epistemology may need to be downed.

At the level of the deep structures of the 'grammar of a school' (Tyack and Cuban, 1995), the relationship schools have to knowledge, engagement and creation is challenged when contemplative practices and atmospheres become part of what makes a school and teaching work. This idea of the potential of silence as contemplative thinking has compatibilities with theoretical work being done with complex 'emergence'. Silence does not offer a pre-existing world and 'emergence' calls forth the possibility of not entering into one (see Osberg and Biesta, 2007). What silence can offer is the practical and cognitive power to loosen the grip of epistemological ossification in schools. It creates and is a space, a contemplative stance and an energy for new emergences (Huey-li, 2001; Picard, 2002; von Wright, 2012).

A reconfigured reconnection to most current pedagogical practices would allow for oppression to be challenged on a number of significant levels:

Because Western discourses have essentialised mind as the mark of the human and have claimed that its fullest development is to be found among the members of dominant elites (males, whites, upper classes), and because those discourses have severed the functions of the mind from other aspects of human experience, the critique and dissolution of the mind/body binarism are a root issue not only for theoretical holistic pedagogy but also for feminist and other antioppressive theory and praxis. (Orr, 2002:480)

Thinking in and through silence practices in schools could address some of the problems with epistemological injustice that extends beyond the school gates by '... loosen[ing] attachment to dualistic and essentialised thinking and consequently to the destructive ways of living that all cultures produce in their members' (Orr, 2002:486).

Transcendence of the intellectual

Because schooling is expected to develop the intellect, one might think this is what it is about. But many children do not find that intellectual work suits them and would prefer more practical matters. Instead of pursuing academic work they consider their lives best spent in labour to do with the hands rather than only the mind (Watts and Bridges, 2004). The structures of schools are, however, ordered to create intellectual pursuits for assessment purposes. It is these which justify a school's existence and support its claims to excellence:

... a foundational relation with assessment organises contemporary education. Assessment is not something that accompanies education as an additional – sometimes lamented, but somehow necessary – supplement. On the contrary, in our view the principle of assessment is an outward manifestation of the dominant 'principle of reason' – 'nothing is without reason' – that drives and organises the thinking, the material practices and the structures of contemporary education ... (Flint and Peim, 2007:343)

Some people feel this approach to schools has gone too far. Many parents opt to place their children in less driven and means-end oriented educational environments, where personal emotions are valued and wandering and wondering are possible (Lees, 2011; Mintz and Ricci, 2010). Schools orientated towards the intellectual and the linearly cognitive seldom value children who are not suited to these demands.

Silence as a feature of a school landscape can offer the transcendence of the intellectual, but without destruction of the possible importance of the intellectual. This power to offer both transcendence and respect is part of the gentleness of silence. Schools can widen towards a spiritual, psychological and emotional position of greater inclusion without losing their position in league tables. The space for this is found in the silence of the school.

Silence is a practical tool: by sitting in silence, being with silence, entering into silence, the intellectual building work to succeed for assessment and means-end goals is no longer all that matters. The mind can open into spaces which were blocked, circumscribed and determined by structured mental activity. Furthermore, the energy released for building that engagement with silence allows the potential of the individual to emerge. The mind becomes fresh, efficient, steady and humble; less demanding. Ways of thinking such as intuition take on new importance, also faith (Kierkegaard, 1985). New worlds are invited in by silence, many of them more 'spiritual' or moral in nature than those afforded by a mechanistically oriented mindset.

Silence in schools as difference

Assessments, panopticon and 'improvements' are taking over schooled life (Peim and Flint, 2012). The fast pace of the information age is glamorous, whereas silence is not and has no colour. It's quite boring compared to the latest gadget. Silence is slow, contrary to today's 'culture of speed' (Tomlinson, 2007). It is useless, changeless and non-judgemental (Picard, 2002). Bringing silence into schools is a radical move towards difference from the current contextualisation of schools within an information age and its troubled terrain (Lyotard, 1984; Baudrillard, 2004b).

Is it a responsibility of schools to give children options? Do these options allow pupils not to be fast, not be improved, not be assessed? Is it in the interests of children and adults to rarely be still or *not* know that stillness and silence is a personal option? The teacher speaking as UK5 (see chapter 3) mentions that children he worked with for mindfulness awareness talked about how they were amazed to discover that their minds could be observed and stilled (see page 45). Sara Maitland suggests that antisocial behaviour in young people is a result of not knowing about silence:

> I am increasingly persuaded that both the worrying increase in mental health problems and the demonstrations of antisocial, even violent, behaviour in

younger people in the West at present must be related to a lack of silence and a lack of training in how to use silence. (2008:250)

Young people are trapped in a system of being and behaving that does not know the option of silence. So, doing things differently might not make things worse. 'Upsetting the apple cart' might make things better, as it seems to have done through silence in schools in an area of Australia (Day, 2011). But schools are found to be conservative. As Baroness Morris acknowledged, 'little use had been made by schools or local authorities of the power to innovate under the Education Act 2002' (Children Schools and Families Committee, 2010:7).

The headteachers and teachers interviewed for this book spoke about the cumulative effects of silence in schools. This cumulative patience and commitment is an attitude and an investment of time and energy in something that it is hoped will duly bear fruit. This fruit is deemed to be of the 'spirit', but it does not exclude secular approaches. UK6 for instance was only interested in the effect of silence that came from reading quietly, which he saw as special, even awesome – but not religious.

Taking time over silence is important for doing things differently. It is an antidote to rushing into testing, assessment, improvement and the like because its slow nature is a key aspect of resistance. 'Much of the discourse surrounding meditation techniques acknowledges that this process is gradual and staged' (Orr, 2002:488). It changes the school pace, the mind of a school and its spirit.

Readjusting one's speed and opening oneself to a different way of seeing is a process which must be learnt (eg. see Parks, 2010a). Berryman suggests that this process might require a 'reawakening' and 'a shock' to 'participate deeply in the world around ... to connect with the world and to know it personally' and to return to the uncluttered 'original vision' of childhood (Berryman, 1999:265). This is what silence in schools would seem to demand: a strong and shocking change from a schooling modality with only fast-operating mechanisms.

The schools investigated in chapter two already have a basis of difference underpinning their philosophies to facilitate silence as difference. It has been recognised that doing things differently in education might require some form of 'gestalt switch' (Biesta, 1994:317) or 'turning point' (Mintz and Ricci, 2010). A study I made of what happens to adults when they discover forms of educational alternatives, such as elective home education, showed that a strong move of the self occurs that is identified as a change of paradigm or a conversion into another lifestyle. It is a personal journey involving a leap towards a different and life altering change in perceptions (Lees, 2011). In educational practice it seems that having a fixed mindset might cement the mind and the self into self-defeating cycles of repetition. Educational changes might require a strong, drastic switch to do things differently. Or it could be that introducing silence into schools sets in train, an ethos or ecology of small moments that cumulatively and together impact powerfully, so that one day, suddenly, things seem different.

The power of silence for democratic outcomes

Max Picard wrote an intriguing book on silence in which he makes the important observation: 'Silence gives to things inside it something of the power of its own autonomous being. The autonomous being in things is strengthened in silence' (Picard, 2002:19). What Picard recognises is something I too have recognised as occurring through silence in schools: the strengthening of democratic experiences and possibilities.

Much has been written about the theoretical and practical problem of how to introduce greater democracy into schools (eg. Gutmann, 2008; Biesta, 2006; Harber, 2004; Trafford, 2003; Crick, 1998). The lack of structural and systemic democracy is connected to the student's lack of understanding of what living and contributing to a democratic society means or should mean. Schools are trying to fill the gap in children's knowledge about being political. Peim and Flint (2012) among others argue that these efforts are doomed to fail, because schooling is institutionally, historically and socially set up to be anti-democratic. Yet many strive for more democratically inclined structures (eg. Fielding and Moss, 2010) and 'deepening democracy in a fragmented world' (UNDP, 2002).

Fully democratic schools are usually independent schools which are run along philosophical lines of child-freedom and emotional openness, such as Summerhill School in Suffolk and Sands School in Devon, UK, and Sudbury School in the United States (Neill, 1968; Gribble, 2001; Sudbury Valley School, 1992). These schools give an equal vote to each member of the school community – regardless of age or role – when deciding most issues as they affect the school. They allow the students to self-determine their learning styles, patterns, pace and general content. In both the literature about 'contemplative' education and in the schools I visited where a whole school ethos is in place, problems of hierarchy and power are noticeably less dominant. That is not to say there is no hierarchy or power, but there seem to be fewer problems connected to the authoritarian power structures that hierarchies support. What is interesting is that the schools which are not structured democratically, but where silence is a feature, seem to be and behave with greater democracy. Empirical and theoretical research is required to determine if there is a connection and why. But what we do know indicates why silence would influence schools towards greater democratic functioning.

The ethics of tolerance
Schools suffer from the intolerance of otherness that is a common feature of being human. In societies across the globe, people disrespect, disregard and fight with each other over matters such as race, lifestyle and sexuality. Children often express these 'adult' issues in schools as bullying (Glover *et al*, 2000, Marr and Field, 2001; Walton, 2005; Staff Writer, 2008; Bloom, 2009).

In *Silence as Yoga*, Swami Paramananda suggests that 'It is good for us to get away from ourselves, to forget the physical self with its name and form and littleness ...' (Paramananda, 1974:48-49). He advocates a culture and practice of silence to help take people away from superficial concerns. Jon Kabat-Zinn is suggesting something similar when he recommends mindfulness practice to release the mind from bodily and psychological stress (Kabat-Zinn, 2011). A symposium at the Garrison Institute on the future of contemplative education identified two aspects of the 'value added' silence practices can offer, which highlight democratic inclinations: 'a world-view based on interdependence' and 'a view of 'basic humanness" that elicits compassion for all people regardless of differences' (Garrison Institute, 2008:5).

Silence practices recalibrate the order of one's focus, releasing the mind from its attachment to worries and anxieties and allowing it to flow freely. An uncluttered mind is purified of distorted perceptions and a smudged understanding of the self and others. Awareness rests better in a state of calm. Silence dispels the fog in the mind. People in schools who have silence to rest in are less likely to bully or be intolerant (Erricker and Erricker, 2001) because:

■ they are more relaxed and in tune with themselves so are more secure

■ they are more aware of the common and shared humanity of those around them of which they are one element

■ they are more aware of the contents of their minds so their reactions and impulses are more controlled.

The qualitative accounts cited in this book broadly concur that such effects seem achievable through silence practices. They echo the poetic views of a century ago: 'Gradually, as mind, soul and even body grow still ... the pettiness, the tangles, the failures of the outer life begin to be seen in their true proportions ...' (Fry, 1910).

The theory is that the mind is *affected* by silence and that this has an impact on interpersonal and personal behaviour. I welcome the interest in a broadly behaviourist perspective on silence in schools elucidated (in time) by the tools of neuroscience. But a good deal of any present or future considerations concerning silence in schools has nothing to do with behaviourism and is rightly resistant to being measured and assessed.

Silence manifests what is promising for democratic interactions: 'fruits of the spirit' or of the 'inner self' include compassion, joy, willingness to listen, ability to listen to others, eyes that see with wisdom and so on. However, a bit of silence does not mean we immediately have tolerance. Silence for democratic outcomes operates through cognitive cause and effect, but also through the *spaces* for self and other that silence offers, wherein democratic possibilities can flourish as interactive, exploratory attitudes. Democracy in schools takes work and time – 'it must be built', as documents discussing how world democracy can become a reality say (UNDP, 2002:4). Silence, as practitioners in chapters two and three suggest, takes work, time and operates through cumulative effects. Silence suits democracy at a functional, structural level and it also fosters changes to interpersonal tolerance and communication. Silence suits democracy. Silence in schools suits democracy in schools.

A 'purer' vision

The 'eyes of judgment' can be cleansed by a vision of silence as a something that is nothingness. Perceiving in silence and experiencing silence is to be in and understand a world with less division, assessment, measurement and pressure to conform.

Hall *et al* (1997) present a social worker's narrative about the young mother whose children were taken into care because of the social worker's actions. They stress that the voices of the mother and her partner and their children are ignored. The story as the social worker tells it shows how the mother did not behave in accordance with his preferred family set-up. The authors analyse his account to show how the authoritative professional voice can fail to tell an accurate story and can never tell the whole story. Disagreeing with the social worker's version of events, a judge returns the children to the mother's care, choosing to not agree with his story. Similar scenarios play themselves out in schools. Children find themselves up against a school's version of what should be, be it with regard to uniform, appearance, behaviour, physical comportment and much else (eg. see Agencies, 2011; Lipsett, 2008; Lees, 2010). Sometimes there are good reasons for sanctions and boundaries on grounds of health and safety. Mostly such rules and regulations are imposed on pupils, who must blindly obey without any say in the matter. However, in silence the authoritative voice is suspended. Children are, if just for a few moments, free of the judgement mechanisms of the school. They are released into relationships that are more fluid. Silence is time out from the authoritarian structures.

Seeing things differently and behaving differently from a set of 'agreed' social and school norms can, if not given a voice, provoke subversion (Willis, 1981; Marsh *et al*, 1978). Disagreeing with school norms but being unable to negotiate the rules of engagement can drive people away, possibly to elective home education (Lees, 2011). This is an example of Hirshmann's theory of 'voice, loyalty, exit', where employees loose loyalty and leave an organisation, if there is no chance to speak out about matters that concern them (Hirschman, 1970). Truancy in schools is often such an exit (Carlen *et al*, 1992). So is much school phobia and refusal (Yoneyama, 2000; Pilkington and Piersel, 1991; Fortune-Wood, 2007). Being 'other' in a school can be harmful for social and personal well-being. Silence as a technology softens the idea of the other.

Silence seems to have an effect on a sense of people being apart and 'other' from each other. Patten developed a module at his university on 'discovering silence' for first year undergraduates, which he taught for six years. He found that the use of silence as the curriculum material for the course levelled the hierarchical power dynamics of education in subtle ways. When an exercise required working in pairs, Patten became one of the students. His students felt empowered to suggest actions, such as sitting for zazen meditation or listening to a particular piece of music to identify pauses. All this created a sense of ownership of the learning experience and the subject matter: 'the students felt that it was *their* course, an especially good thing for university beginners to feel' (Patten, 1997:374 author's emphasis). Patten notes that his course shut the 'professor' up, quoting William James's remark that: 'the natural enemy of any subject is the professor thereof'. Patten observed:

> ... one of the chief things that I discovered in my experience of teaching the course was that students became students of themselves and of how they understood the world, and many of them mentioned exactly this in their evaluations of the course. I knew other things, too, such as that there would be not lectures here, that, if possible I as a teacher must be like the students, a discoverer. (Patten, 1997:370)

Patten considers the hierarchical voice of the textbook as inappropriate to the course: 'there are no textbooks in this field (and if there had been, I would not have used them)' (*op cit*:371). Silence democratises educational experiences for both students and teachers by affecting what is deemed educational. In Patten's experiment both interpersonal relationships and also the transmission of knowledge are affected. His students reported enjoying a reinvigorated relationship to knowledge and a keen sense of personal discovery. They found silence engaging: silent walks; visits to galleries; responses to music and its pauses; staring at photographs; watching silent films. Interestingly, they found the most profound and impactful learning to be in their practices of zazen meditative sitting. Patten's experiment illustrates the democratisation of education through silence practices. Democratisation develops naturally and becomes necessary to silence:

There was no way that I could avoid being a leader, in the sense that I had to give them weekly assignments, but I always would try to assign them projects which I myself would have to do, with as little sense of what they would lead to as they had. If the course was going to succeed, I had to walk in the same darkness of my eighteen year olds. (Patten, 1997:370)

Although this took place with university undergraduates, the theory, spirit and practice could equally apply to school-age children.

The mechanisms and activities of the mind behave differently in and through silence. This can allow for relations in school settings to change. Relations are freer; they are less pressured by school expectations. They can withstand the demands from outside that make people feel a need to conform, because silence as an epistemological framework is less divided.

Nataraja (2008) asserts that silence can be a mechanism by which the different hemispheres of the brain can 'come together' and operate harmoniously. This effect of 'coming together' also brings people together in the material world. This was noted in reports of meditation programmes in prisons or educational referral units that lacked inter-personal tolerance and understanding and had worked along strict lines of hierarchy and authority before the silence practices were introduced (Abrams and Siegel, 1978; Macleish, 2009; Dye, 2001).

The effect of silence might create greater possibilities for democratic atmosphere and behaviour in schools. Silence can transform blunt authoritarianism and this promotes inter-personal harmony, allowing people to become calmer individuals. This, then, promotes greater silence and the replacement of authoritarian structures with constructive relationships (Bingham, 2008).

While talk and debate must always be a part of democracy in a school, silence enhances the atmosphere within which debate occurs. The mental and emotional clarity that emerges from silence practices, especially when they are long-standing, contributes to democratic development in schools. Schools, driven by content delivery, can fall into an excess of information stimulus, which may provoke a new uncertainty:

... it is a question here of a completely new species of uncertainty, which results not from the *lack* of information but from information itself and even from an excess of information. (Baudrillard, 2004a:213, original emphasis)

The uncertainty of knowing too much is stressful. The modern world offers a double bind of needing discourse to feel safe, whilst feeling unsure because of too much discourse:

> ... general benumbment is such as cannot tolerate silence; it needs the reassuring pulse of music or background chatter ... it is evident in the therapeutic inclination to annul the space between people in a kind of communicative sociability, to chat and make people feel at home ... the orientation towards discourse offers a greater sense of cognitive security and far fewer demands. (Blake *et al*, 2000:149)

As Jean Baudrillard observes: 'we are no longer confronted with our own will' and 'the situation no longer permits us to isolate reality or human nature as a fundamental variable' (2004a:213). Democracy is needed more than ever because our sense of self in relation to self and other is shattered by discourse and need for discourse. But the lack of inherent social and interpersonal meaning is, according to Baudrillard, 'obscene': 'the social becomes obsessed with itself ... it becomes its own vice, its own perversion. This is the real obscenity'. When 'the present argument of the system is to maximise speech, to maximise the production of meaning, of participation' (*op cit*:222), silence can deliver democracy and democratic understanding that is not overloading children with information.

Silence and neuroscience

Neuroscience has increasingly been considered as having a potential role in education and is being promoted as the scientific saviour of educational anomalies:

> Education is about enhancing learning, and neuroscience is about understanding the mental processes involved in learning. This common ground suggests a future in which educational practice can be transformed by science, just as medical practice was transformed by science about a century ago. (The Royal Society, 2011)

However, not everyone agrees that 'education is [just] about enhancing learning' (eg. Biesta, 2006).

Plasticity in the brain's internal structures means that cognitive modification can be achieved through tailored mind-focused programmes (Doidge, 2007; Begley, 2009). In light of this, Catherine Malabou asks:

'What should we do with our brain?' (2008). The idea of neuro-tinkering brings with it a whole raft of possible ethical and social questions. Will education which functions according to neuroscientific principles be more equal? How will it work and will its workings require access to be facilitated for everybody, or only to the privileged few? Is neuroscience going to show us that we don't need the structures of schools? Will it re-inforce the power of schools for the delivery of the scientifically proven 'best' way? There is much optimism over the potential for neuroscience to support education. But what effects might the introduction of neuro-science into education have for the democratic treatment of children? Here I argue that silence is golden.

The neurological effect of techniqued and technique-less silence prac-tices may, on ethical and moral grounds, be the safest intervention to create cognitive modification. Without the use of language, words and expectations prescribed by research, the 'holy uselessness' of silence (Picard, 2002) takes on its own world of benefit. According to Wittgen-stein (1992) language is generative of 'forms of life' such that words create worlds. It is the very inability of silence to prescribe a world, be-cause it has not tools of language with which to do that, that benefits education. A mix of neuroscience and language in education can lead to the kinds of determinism towards learning efficacy as a 'holy grail' that some educationists believe distorts educational purpose (Biesta, 2006).

Silence practices can cognitively adapt the brain (Nataraja, 2008). In schools this could allow for enhanced brain function and enhanced learning potential that can *avoid* such prescription. The fundamental freedom of the self and the mind that silence offers is a safe neurologi-cal intervention in this regard. It is therefore an enabler of the demo-cratic in that what is decided, what occurs and what is chosen happen internally, silently. Silence is not coercive – there is no 'mission of truth' (Lacan, 1973) – so the truths that belong to a community can evolve and emerge through the use of silence. This democratic effect is facilitated by the power of silence to interact with the brain's plasticity, producing what I call a golden effect of silence in schools.

Undoing externalisation of the self

Externalisation of the self is a natural part of human life. It is a part of the construction of 'the world *into* which man externalises himself. In the process of externalisation, he projects his own meanings into reality' (Berger and Luckmann, 1966:121-122). But children who grow up not realising that they have an internal world into which they can 'internalise' themselves lack the tools to manage themselves. They would have no happy art of self creation (Foucault, 1986). Schools are not good at promoting the idea that humans have an interior world. Rewarding good behaviour, focusing on learning for means-end goals, encouraging competition all contribute to a focus on external gratifications which can overwhelm a centring within:

> ... the present educational system that we have is actually imprisoning the brains of our children. By focusing on the very important skills that we all learn: reading, writing and arithmetic, but not on another set of R's which I will suggest ... all schools need to do is to look at reflection, relationships and resilience. And we now have the technology ... to promote a different kind of brain growth, because now what's happening ... is we have a damaged brain that's growing and it's getting more and more handicapped as kids get more focused on the external world rather than being able to look at the internal world ... (Siegel, 2009)

Silence in schools might help children to escape the idea of performance for reward, of being beholden to forces outside of oneself or simply a belief that what matters in life is external to inner experience. Dauenhauer writes about this interventionist power of silence:

> Silence is a founded, active performance which, in its pure occurrences, does not directly intend an already fully determinate object of any sort. Rather, ... motivated by finitude and awe, silence interrupts or cuts an already instituted stream of intentional performances which in most cases, intend determinate objects. (Dauenhauer, 1980:140)

In other words, silence can bring you back to yourself through an awareness that is felt internally and which is sufficiently attractive to reorient the locus of attention. This replaces a focus tending towards outside objects, events and aims with an internal arena in which to 'indwell', fed by emotions of awe and wonder. Such 'indwelling' (a term borrowed here for connections to Polanyi's meaning of immersion (1974, 1983) causes reflective tendencies to be privileged and enjoyed. Contemplation, whilst not necessarily easy, is a pleasure (Merton, 1974).

Silence gains power by having no identifiable attainment as reward. It has no part of a competitive environment with its adrenalin rushes of winning and losing. No comparisons are made – the practice of meditation or mindfulness is removed from all notions of streaming, league tables, testing, assessment or measuring. This can be a challenging shift in perspective for children who have come to expect that they will be placed in some kind of hierarchy of achievement. The absence of comparison and assessment can become an equaliser in the child's mind but also within the community of others who have differing abilities, developmental pace and skills. 'Success' in silence practices is of an inner kind and this dims the focus on external gratification. Studies considering meditation as an aid to reducing external addictions show it to be effective (Pruett *et al*, 2007). For children who react to external stimuli with hyperactivity and lack of concentration, meditative practices bring them back to their centre and can reduce symptoms of ADHD (Harrison *et al*, 2004; Grosswald *et al*, 2008).

If children are feeling less competitive in schools because they are chilled out by having dwelt in silence, they become the radicals of rebellion against heirarchical control by literally – for a chosen moment – doing nothing. Silence in schools sets in place messages for children that there is another possible school culture to experience than the pressure to succeed.

> These students ... realise that they are caught in a system where achievement depends more on 'doing' – going through the correct motions – than on learning and engaging with the curriculum. Instead of thinking deeply about the content of their courses and delving into projects and assignments, the students focus on managing the workload and honing strategies that will help them to achieve high grades ... As Kevin asserts:
>
>> 'People don't go to school to learn. They go to get good grades which brings them to college, which brings them the high-paying job, which brings them to happiness so they think. But basically, grades is where it's at.' (Pope, 2001)

In an otherwise saturated environment of externalisation, silence is a treasure for schools. When children say they are stressed by a need to attain, they are not exhibiting satisfaction and pleasure with their schooling experience.

The *Guardian's* report in 2011 of a talk given by two educationists in Queensland Australia, sums up the arguments made in this chapter:

> When an almost pathological 'busyness' is the norm, valuing stillness and silence is counter-cultural. When our culture trains us to be winners, to compete and to consume, we all sense society's imbalance, said Freeman. We need to give children an experience of another way of relating to themselves and to others. Deputy director Christie agreed. If children are over-stimulated we rob them of something precious: being allowed to 'just be' where children discover their own inner sense of who they are. Hijacked by a 'doing' culture that measures everything by what we achieve or possess, meditation helps children access a deeper part of themselves – an inner sanctuary away from a world of incessant activity and noise. They learn to honour their own spiritual life. (Lancaster, 2011)

Conclusion

This chapter considers three key powers that silence can bring to school settings. The testimonies in chapter two suggest that the practice of silence contributes to successful and happy schools. Investigating how theory and practice coalesce for all schools is only beginning.

As I have discussed and as the educationists who work with silence have reported, silence is not an obedient servant, directed to perform whatever 'transformation' a school may require. Silence demands humility in its users: no-one can command silence to behave in a certain way. It puts people in their place, but not a place in a hierarchy. The powers of silence in schools do not belong to those with power. They just are.

Silence in schools strips away falsity and allows for a parrhesia, a frankness of truth-telling, to occur (Foucault, 2001). Being able to think differently, being amongst other people as equals, being able to resort to inner resources of the self through awareness of reflective abilities, are each and all powerful contributions to school life. It could be that in this astonishing 'nothing' lies what schools need to fulfil their educational and social promises to their pupils.

7

Silence after all ...

This book is a research project and an exercise in communication – so it has used words. The interviews with the headteachers and teachers show that talking about how silence functions or could function in a school is key. Talking about silence helps it be seen as a resource for schools which is worth the effort. The people who do engage with silence in schools experience the value and their accounts may encourage others to make the effort required to enter into silence. To be with silence as experience is everything.

Consequently I choose to symbolise and point towards silence with this concluding chapter in a radical way. It may be a sacrifice, but it is one that I believe in. I have used talk and the words of others to make effects which can help us understand better, engage better and be more interested in the phenomenon of silence in schools. But I cannot talk about what is beyond words.

The conclusion to a book on silence in schools can appropriately be about silence on terms that are silent, not worded. It is possible to open things up now to the subject matter at hand in experiential terms. I have decided that to not write here a conventional overview of what I have said in previous chapters is to move authentically to the something that all the people featured in this book – including me – are talking about. We really do mean silence.

So there is no conclusion other than the one that you, the reader, find for yourself. I leave the conclusion to you because it may be created by silence and made of it. If it is not, at least I have created space for the possibility.

I will not fill this space of a conclusion chapter to tie up the book, or my thoughts, or silence. I leave it open: to honour the fact that the beauty and value of silence in schools *in action* is not about talking.

References

Abrams, A. I. and Siegel, L. M. (1978) The Transcendental Meditation® Program and Rehabilitation at Folsom State prison: a cross-validation study. *Criminal Justice and Behavior* 5(1) p3-20

Agencies (2011) School's refusal to let boy wear cornrow braids is ruled racial discrimination. *The Guardian*, 17.06.11

Alerby, E. (2012) *Om tystnad – i pedagogiska sammanhang* [About Silence – in educational settings]. Lund: Studentlitteratur

Alexander, R. (2009) Children, their World, their Education: final report and recommendations of the Cambridge Primary Review. Cambridge: Routledge

Anderson, V. L., Levinson, E. M., Barker, W. and Kiewra, K. R. (1999) The effects of meditation on teacher perceived occupational stress, state and trait anxiety, and burnout. *School Psychology Quarterly* 14(1) p3-25

Andrieu, B. (ed.) (2003) *Corps, Peau, Silences, dans L'enseignement*, Nancy: CRDP de Lorraine

Anglo European School (2012) *The sanctuary*. URL: http://aesessex.regulus.titaninter net.co.uk/pages.asp?Pageid=161: [30.05.12]

Apple, M. W. (1995) What post-modernists forget: cultural capital and official knowledge. *School Field* 6(3-4) p47-65

Appleton, M. (2002) *Summerhill: a free range childhood*. Loughton: Gale Centre Publications

Arendt, H. (2006) *Eichmann in Jerusalem*. London: Penguin Books

Baer, R. A. (2003) Mindfulness training as a clinical intervention: a conceptual and empirical review. *American Psychological Association* 10(2) p125-143

Barker, I. (2009) Quietly does it as Quakers look back to the future. *The Times Educational Supplement*, 08.01.09

Barnes, V. A., Davis, H. C., Murzynowski, J. B. and Treiber, F. A. (2004) Impact of meditation on resting and ambulatory blood pressure and heart rate in youth. *Psychosomatic Medicine* 66 p909-914

Baudrillard, J. (1993) *Symbolic Exchange and Death*. London: Sage

Baudrillard, J. (2004a) The masses: the implosion of the social in the media. In: Poster, M. (ed.) *Jean Baudrillard – Selected writings.* Cambridge: Polity Press

Baudrillard, J. (2004b) Symbolic exchange and death. In: Poster, M. (ed.) *Jean Baudrillard – Selected writings.* Cambridge: Polity Press

Baudrillard, J. and Guillaume, M. (2008) *Radical Alterity.* Los Angeles: Semiotext(e)

Begley, S. (2009) *The Plastic Mind.* London: Constable and Robinson Ltd

Begley, S. (2011) I Can't Think! *Newsweek,* 27.02.11

Begoray, D. and Bannister, E. M. (2008) Wonder and Danger: knowledge translation and indigeneous adolescent girls' sexual health education in indigenous communities. University of Birmingham: Invited Lecture sponsored by Faculty of Education

Bennis, D. M. and Graves, I. R. (eds.) (2007) *The Directory of Democratic Education,* USA: Alternative Education Resource Organisation

BERA (2004) *Revised Ethical Guidelines for Educational Research.* Macclesfield: British Educational Research Association

Berger, P. L. and Luckmann, T. (1966) *The Social Construction of Reality: a treatise in the sociology of knowledge.* Garden City, NY: Anchor Books

Berryman, J. W. (1999) Silence is stranger than it used to be: teaching silence and the future of humankind. *Religious Education* 94(3)

Biesta, G. J. J. (1994) Education as practical intersubjectivity: towards a critical-pragmatic understanding of education. *Educational Theory* 44(3) p299-317

Biesta, G. J. J. (2006) *Beyond Learning: Democratic education for a human future.* London: Paradigm Publishers

Biesta, G. J. J. (2007) Why 'what works' won't work. Evidence-based practice and the democratic deficit of educational research. *Educational Theory* 57(1) p1-22

Biesta, G. J. J. (2008) Pedagogy with empty hands: Levinas, education and the question of being human. In: Egéa-Kuehne, D. (ed.) *Levinas and Education At the Intersection of Faith and Reason.* London: Routledge

Biesta, G. J. J. (2009) Good education in an age of measurement: on the need to reconnect with the question of purpose in education. *Educational Assessment, Evaluation and Accountability* 21(1) p33-46

Biesta, G. J. J. (2010) *Good Education in an Age of Measurement: ethics, politics, democracy.* Boulder, CO: Paradigm Publishers

Biesta, G. J. J. (2011) Disciplines and theory in the academic study of education: a comparative analysis of the Anglo-American and Continental construction of the field. *Pedagogy, Culture and Society* 19(2) p175-192

Bingham, C. (2008) *Authority is Relational.* Albany: State University of New York Press

Blake, N., Smeyers, P., Smith, R. and Standish, P. (2000) *Education in an Age of Nihilism.* London and New York: Routledge Falmer

Bloom, A. (2009) Racist bullying rife in schools, says poll. *Times Educational Supplement,* 24.04.09

Bolte Taylor, J. (2008) *My Stroke of Insight.* London: Hodder and Stoughton

Bowles, S. and Gintis, H. (1976) *Schooling in Capitalist America.* London: Routledge and Kegan Paul

Brady, R. (2007) Learning to stop, stopping to learn. *Journal of Transformative Education* 5(4) p372-394

Brand, R. (2011) A letter from Russell Brand to you the reader. URL: http://www.crowdrise.com/supportmeditation/fundraiser/russellbrand: [16/04/11]

Breton, P. and Breton, D. L. (2009) *Le Silence et la Parole: Contre les excès de la communication.* Strasbourg: Éditions Érès

Brown, L. and Coles, A. (2008) *Hearing Silence: Steps to teaching mathematics.* Cambridge: Black Apollo Press

Bruneau, T. (1973) Communicative silences: forms and functions. *The Journal of Communication* 23 p17-46

Burke, C. A. (2010) Mindfulness-based approaches with children and adolescents: a preliminary review of current research in an emergent field. *Journal of Child and Family Studies* 19(2) p133-144

Burnett, R. (2009) *Mindfulness in Schools: Learning lessons from the adults – secular and Buddhist.* MA, Sunderland University

Cage, J. (1961) *Silence: Lectures and Writings.* Middletown, CT: Wesleyan University Press

Campion, J. (2009) Minding the mind: the effects and potential of a school-based meditation programme for mental health promotion. *Advances in School Mental Health Promotion* 2(1) p47-55

Campion, J. (2011) A review of the research on meditation. *The Meditatio Journal* Autumn(1) p29-37

Capra, F. (1990) The crisis of perception. *The Futurist* 24(1)

Caranfa, A. (2004) Silence as the Foundation of Learning. *Educational Theory* 54(2)

Carlen, P., Gleeson, D. and Wardhaugh, J. (1992) *Truancy: The politics of complusory schooling.* Buckingham: Open University Press

Castagno, A. E. (2008) 'I don't want to hear that!': Legitimating whiteness through silence in schools. *Anthropology and Education Quarterly* 39(3) p314-333

Chaudron, C. (1988) *Second Language Classroom: Research on teaching and learning.* Cambridge: Cambridge University Press

Children Schools and Families Committee (2010) From Baker to Balls: the foundations of the education system, Ninth Report of Session 2009-10. London: House of Commons

Clair, R. P. (1998) *Organising Silence: a world of possibilities.* Albany: State University of New York Press

Clay, D. (2009) Curriculum – Sounds creative. *Times Educational Supplement,* 04.12.09

Codacci Pisanelli, A. (2010) Gli amanti del silenzio. *L'espresso*, 08.04.10

Condliffe Lagemann, E. (2002) *An Elusive Science: The troubling history of education research*. Chicago: University Of Chicago Press

Cooper, D. E. (2008) Powers of silence. *Kristiansand seminar presentation notes*.

Cooper, D. E. (2012) Silence, nature and education. In: Kristiansen, A. and Hägg, H. (eds.) *Attending to Silence*. Norway: Portal

Crick, B. (1998) *Education for Citizenship and the Teaching of Democracy in Schools: Final report of the advisory group on citizenship*. London: QCA

Csikszentmihalyi, M. (2008) *Flow: the Psychology of Optimal Experience*. New York: Harper Perrenial

Curry, W. B. (1947) *Education for Sanity*. London: Heinemann

Curtis, P. (2008) Homophobic abuse endemic in schools, says teacher survey. *The Guardian*, 11.03.08

Daily Mail Reporter (2010) Goldie Hawn in talks with Tories to set up British school which teaches children breathing exercises. *The Daily Mail*, 14.02.10

Dauenhauer, B. P. (1980) *Silence: the phenomenon and its ontological significance*. Bloomington: Indiana University Press

David Lynch Foundation (2007) 'Catching the Big Fish' comes to Ireland and the UK 20-27 October. URL: http://www.consciousnessbasededucation.org.uk/images/PRLynch-DonovanUK-IrelandTour19-27October.pdf: [17 July 2011]

Davidson, R. J., Kabat-Zinn, J., Schumacher, J., Rosenkranz, M., Muller, D., Santoralli, S. F., Urbanowski, F., Harrington, A., Bonus, K. and Sheridan, J. F. (2003) Alterations in brain and immune function produced by mindfulness meditation. *Psychosomatic Medicine* 65(4) p564-570

Day, C. (2011) Let's be daring and upset the apple cart. *The Meditatio Journal* Autumn(1)

DCSF (2008) National strategies, early years. every child a talker: guidance for early language lead practitioners. In: *Department for Children Schools and Families* (ed.). Nottingham: DCSF Publications

de Smedt, M. (1986) *Éloge du Silence*. Paris: Albin Michel

Delandshere, G. (2001) Implict theories, unexamined assumptions and the status quo of educational assessment. *Assessment in Education* 8(2)

Deleuze, G. and Guattari, F. (2004) *A Thousand Plateaus*. London: Continuum

Dewey, J. (1960) *A Common Faith*. New Haven: Yale University Press

Doidge, N. (2007) *The Brain that Changes Itself*. London: Penguin

Doll, W. E. (1993) *A Post-modern Perspective on Curriculum*. New York: Teachers College Press

Dowty, T. (2000) *Free Range Education: how home education works*. Stroud: Hawthorn Press

Dye, J. (2001) Introducing meditation to young people with behavioural and emotional difficulties. In: Erricker, C. and Erricker, J. (eds.) *Meditation in Schools*. London: Continuum

Ecclestone, K. and Hayes, D. (2009) *The Dangerous Rise of Therapeutic Education*. Abingdon: Routledge

Echeverria, E. and Hannam, P. (2009) *Philosophy with Teenagers: nurturing a moral imagination for the 21st century*. London: Continuum

Eco Schools (2011) *Peace away from the main playground*. URL: http://www.eco-schools.org.uk/assets/uploaded/resources/50_CS%20-%20Norton%20Primary%20School.pdf: [31.07.11]

Ephratt, M. (2008) The functions of silence. *Journal of Pragmatics* 40 p1909-1938

Erricker, C. and Erricker, J. (eds.) (2001) *Meditation in Schools: calmer classrooms*, London Continuum

Farrer, F. (2000) *A Quiet Revolution: encouraging positive values in our children*. London: Rider

Fielding, M. (2010) Whole school meetings and the development of radical democratic community. *Studies in Philosophy and Education online first* phttp://www.springerlink.com/content/q01u4127236344n3/

Fielding, M. and Moss, P. (2010) *Radical Education and the Common School: A democratic alternative*. London: Routledge

Fine, M. (1987) Silencing in public schools. *Language Arts* 64(2)

Flint, K. and Peim, N. (2007) *Testing Times: questions concerning assessment for school improvement*. Nottingham Trent University and University of Birmingham

Fontaine, J. (1997) The sound of silence: public school response to the needs of gay and lesbian youth. In: Harris, M. B. (ed.) *School Experiences of Gay and Lesbian Youth: the invisible minority*. Binghampton, NY: The Haworth Press

Fonteneau, F. (1999) *L'éthique du Silence: Wittgenstein et Lacan*. Paris: Éditions du Seuil

Forbes, S. H. (2000) *Jiddu Krishnamurti and his insights into education*. URL: http://www.infed.org/thinkers/et-krish.htm: [17.08.11]

Forrest, M. (2010) Practising silence in a community of inquiry. *Philosophy of Education Society Great Britain Conference*. New College, Oxford:

Fortune-Wood, M. (2007) *Can't Go Won't Go: an alternative approach to school refusal*. Blaenau Ffestiniog: Cinnamon Press

Foucault, M. (1977) *Discipline and Punish*. London: Penguin

Foucault, M. (1986) *The Care of the Self – The history of sexuality: vol 3*. London: Penguin

Foucault, M. (1988) Technologies of the self. In: Martin, L., Gutman, H. and Hutton, P. (eds.) *Technologies of the Self*. London: Tavistock

Foucault, M. (1998) *The History of Sexuality: Volume 1*. London: Penguin

Foucault, M. (2001) *Fearless Speech*. Los Angeles: Semiotext

Foucault, M. (2002) *The Order of Things*. Abingdon, Oxon: Routledge

Foucault, M. (2004) *Abnormal: lectures at the College de France, 1974-1975*. New York: Picador

Fox News (2009) *Illinois Moment of Silence in Schools Ruled Unconstitutional*. URL: http://www.foxnews.com/story/0,2933,481427,00.html: [31.07.11]

Foy, G. M. (2010) *Zero Decibels: The quest for absolute silence*. New York: Scribner

Foy, G. M. (2012) Experience: I've been to the quietest place on Earth. *The Guardian*, 19.05.12

Friere, P. (1972) *Pedagogy of the Oppressed*. Harmondsworth: Penguin

Fry, J. M. (1910) The Communion of Life: Swarthmore lectures. *Quakers' 'London Yearly Meeting'*.

Fuller, B. and Snyder, C. W. (1991) Vocal teachers, silent pupils? Life in Botswana classrooms. *Comparative Education Review* 35(2)

Garrison Institute (2008) Envisioning the future of contemplative education: Garrison Institute Symposium Comprehensive Report. http://www.garrisoninstitute.org/index. php?option=com_content&view=category&layout=blog&id=126&Itemid=91:The Garrison Institute

Gilligan, C. and Brown, L. M. (1993) *Meeting at the Crossroads*. New York: Random House

Gilmore, P. (1985) Silence and sulking: emotional displays in the classroom. In: Tannen, D. and Saville-Troike, M. (eds.) *Perspectives on Silence*. Norwood, NJ: Ablex Publishing Corporation

Glenn, C. (2004) *Unspoken: a rhetoric of silence*. Carbondale: Southern Illinois Press

Glover, D., Gough, G., Johnson, M. and Cartwright, N. (2000) Bullying in 25 secondary schools: incidence, impact and intervention. *Educational Research* 42(2) p141-156

Go, N. (2008) *Les Printemps du Silence*. Paris: Buchet Chastel

Gold, E., Smith, A., Hopper, L., Herne, D., Tansey, G. and Hulland, C. (2009) Mind-fulness-Based Stress Reduction (MBSR) for primary school teachers. *Journal of Child and Family Studies* 19(2) p184-189

Goodsman, D. (1992) *Summerhill: theory and practice*. Ph.D., East Anglia

Gribble, D. (2001) *Worlds Apart*. London: Libertarian Education

Grosswald, S. J., Stixrud, W. R., Travis, F. and Bateh, M. A. (2008) Use of the Trans-cendental Meditation technique to reduce symptoms of Attention Deficit Hyperactivity Disorder (ADHD) by reducing stress and anxiety: an exploratory study. *Current Issues in Education* [On-line] 10(2)

Gurdjieff, G. I. (1984 edition) *Views from the Real World: Early talks*. London: Penguin, Arkana

Gutmann, A. (2008) Democracy and democratic education. In: Curren, R. (ed.) *Philo-sophy of Education: an anthology*. Oxford: Blackwell Publishing

Haines, M. M., Stansfeld, S. A., Job, R. F. S., Berglund, B. and Head, J. (2001) Chronic aircraft noise exposure, stress responses, mental health and cognitive performance in school children. *Psychological Medicine* 31 p265-277

Hall, C., Srangi, S. and Slembrouck, S. (1997) Silent and silenced voices: interactional construction of audience in social work talk. In: Jaworski, A. (ed.) *Silence: interdisciplinary perspectives*. Berlin and New York: Mouton de Gruyter

Hanson, R. and Mendius, R. (2009) *Buddha's Brain*. Oakland, CA: New Harbinger Publications

Harber, C. (2004) *Schooling as Violence: how schools harm pupils and societies.* London: Routledge Falmer

Harrison, L. J., Manocha, R. and Rubia, K. (2004) Sahaja Yoga Meditation as a family treatment programme for children with Attention Deficit-Hyperactivity Disorder. *Clinical Child Psychology and Psychiatry* 9(4) p479-497

Hart, T. (2004) Opening the contemplative mind in the classroom. *Journal of Transformative Education* 2(1) p28-46

Hartley, D. (2008) Personalisation: the nostalgic revival of child-centred education? *Journal of Education Policy* 24(4) p423-434

Haskins, C. (2010) Integrating silence practices into the classroom: the value of quiet. *Encounter: Education for Meaning and Social Justice* 23(3)

Hastings, R. P. and Singh, N. N. (2010) Editorial: mindfulness, children, and families. *Journal of Child and Family Studies* 19 p131-132

Hawn, G. (2011) *Goldie Hawn on Giving TV.* URL: http://www.youtube.com/watch?v =zggFzTkGQgs: [08.01.12]

Hayes, R. and Matusov, E. (2005) Designing for dialogue in place of teacher talk and student silence. *Culture and Psychology* 11(3) p339-357

Hempton, G. and Grossman, J. (2009) *One Square Inch of Silence: one man's quest to preserve quiet.* New York: Free Press

Hirschman, A. O. (1970) *Exit, Voice, and Loyalty.* Cambridge, Massacheusetts: Harvard University Press

Huey-li, L. (2001) Silences and silencing silences. In: PES (ed.) *Philosophy of Education Yearbook.* Philosophy of Education Society

Hunter, A. (1988) *Seeds of truth: J. Krishnamurti as religious teacher and educator.* PhD, University of Leeds

Huppert, F. A. and Johnson, D. M. (2010) A controlled trial of mindfulness training in schools: the importance of practice for an impact on well-being. *Journal of Positive Psychology* 5(4) p264-274

Jaworski, A. (1993) *The Power of Silence.* London: Sage

Jaworski, A. (ed.) (1997) *Silence: Interdisciplinary Perspectives.* Berlin and New York: Mouton de Gruyter

Jaworski, A. and Sachdev, I. (1998) Beliefs about silence in the classroom. *Language and Education* 12(4) p273-292

John Templeton Foundation (2010) 2010 Capabilities Report. West Conshohocken, Pennsylvania: John Templeton Foundationand http://www.templeton.org/sites/default/ files/capabilities_report_ 2010.pdf:

Jullien, F. (2009) *Les Transformations Silencieuses*. Paris: Grasset

Kabat-Zinn, J. (2005) *Coming to Our Senses: healing and the world through mindfulness*. New York: Hyperion

Kabat-Zinn, J. (2011) *Full Catastrophe Living : how to cope with stress, pain and illness using mindfulness meditation*. London: Piatkus

Kalamaras, G. (1994) *Reclaiming the Tacit Dimension*. New York: State University of New York Press

Kay, J. (2011) *Obliquity: Why our goals are best achieved indirectly*. London: Profile Books

Kelley, P. (2008) *Making minds: what's wrong with education, and what should we do about it?* London: Routledge

Kenny, C. (2011) *The Power of Silence*. London: Karnac Books

Kierkegaard, S. (1985) *Fear and Trembling*. London: Penguin

Krishnamurti, J. (1970) *The Only Revolution* URL: http://www.jiddu-krishnamurti.net/ en/the-only-revolution/1969-00-00-jiddu-krishnamurti-the-only-revolution-india-part-3: [18.08.11 web resource without page number]

Kristjansson, K. (2010) Positive psychology and happiness. *Philosophy of Education Society of Great Britain Newsletter*

Kuhn, T. S. (2000) What are scientific revolutions? In: Conant, J. and Haugeland, J. (eds.) *The Road Since Structure: Philosophical Essays, 1970-1993, with an autobiographical interview*. Chicago: Chicago University Press

Kurzon, D. (1998) *Discourse of Silence*. Amsterdam: John Benjamins

Labaree, D. F. (2006) *The Trouble with Ed Schools*. New Haven and London: Yale University Press

Lacan, J. (1973) L'étourdit. *Scilicet* no 4. Paris: Seuil

Lancaster, S. (2011) Children need more meditation and less stimulation. *The Guardian*

Lane, J. (2006) *The Spirit of Silence: making space for creativity*. Dartington, Devon: Green Books

Lardon, M. (2008) *Finding Your Zone: ten core lessons for achieving peak performance in sports and life*. New York: Penguin

Laski, M. (1980) *Everyday Ecstasy: some observations on the possible social effects of major and minor ecstatic experiences in our daily secular lives*. London: Thames and Hudson

Laverty, M. J. (2010) Learning our concepts. *Journal of Philosophy of Education* 43(SI) p27-40

Lawn, M. and Furlong, J. (2011) *Disciplines of Education: their role in the future of education research*. London: Routledge

Lawy, R., Biesta, G., McDonnell, J., Lawy, H. and Reeves, H. (2009) 'The art of democracy': young people's democratic learning in gallery contexts. *British Educational Research Journal* 36(3) p351-365

Le Clair, A. (2009) *Listening beneath the noise.* New York: Harper

Leander, K. M. (2002) Silencing in classroom interaction: producing and relating social spaces. *Discourse Processes* 34(2) p193-235

Lees, H. E. (2010) The Technology of the Democratic in the Personal. Unpublished manuscript

Lees, H. E. (2011) *PhD: the Gateless Gate of home education discovery: what happens to the self of adults upon discovery of the possibility and possibilities of an educational alternative?* http://etheses.bham.ac.uk/1570/. University of Birmingham

Lees, H. E. (2012) Staring at the bird in the tree: 'mind rights' in schools? *Philosophy of Education Society of Great Britain (Edinburgh and Dundee branches) seminar presentation.*

Levete, G. (2001a) Different methods of meditation. In: Erricker, C. and Erricker, J. (eds.) *Meditation in Schools: calmer classrooms.* London: Continuum

Levete, G. (2001b) Meditation as movement: reconnecting with the body. In: Erricker, C. and Erricker, J. (eds.) *Meditation in Schools: calmer classrooms.* London: Continuum

Levete, G. (2001c) Meditation for health and well-being. In: Erricker, C. and Erricker, J. (eds.) *Meditation in Schools: calmer classrooms.* London: Continuum

Levete, G. (2001d) A support for everyday life. In: Erricker, C. and Erricker, J. (eds.) *Meditation in Schools: calmer classrooms.* London: Continuum

Lewis, A. (2010) Silence in the context of 'child voice'. *Children and Society* 24 p14-23

Linden, W. (1973) Practicing of meditation by school children and their levels of field dependence-independence, text anxiety, and reading achievement. *Journal of Consulting and Clinical Psychology* 41(1) p139-143

Lipsett, A. (2008) Sikh schoolgirl wins bangle court case. *The Guardian*, 29.07.08

Lundquist, P., Holmberg, K. and Landstrom, U. (2000) Annoyance and effects on work from environmental noise at school. *Noise and Health* 2(8) p39-46

Lyotard, J.-F. (1984) *The Postmodern Condition: a report on Knowledge.* Manchester: Manchester University Press

Maass, P. (2009) *Crude World: the violent twilight of oil.* London: Allen Lane

Macleish, J. (2009) Meditation transcends difficulties. *Times Educational Supplement,* 07.08.09

Macmurray, J. (1968) [containing papers with dates from 1931 to 1968] Lectures/ Papers on Education. Edinburgh: Edinburgh University Library, Special Collections Gen 2162/2

Maddern, K. (2009) Minister urges headteachers to tackle special needs bullying and exclusions. *Times Educational Supplement*, 20.02.09

Maddern, K. (2011) In the news: Lisa Davies. *Times Educational Supplement,* 24.06.11

Maharishi School (2011) Maharishi School website: home tab. URL: http://www. maharishischool.com/index.html: [07/08/11]

Maitland, S. (2008) *A Book of Silence*. London: Granta

Malabou, C. (2008) *What Should We Do with Our Brain?* New York: Fordham University Press

Mann, C. (2001) The potential of meditation in education. In: Erricker, C. and Erricker, J. (eds.) *Meditation in Schools: calmer classrooms*. Continuum

Mann, C. (2001b) Meditation and the process of learning in education. In: Erricker, C. and Erricker, J. (eds.) *Meditation in Schools: calmer classrooms*. London: Continuum

Marley, D. (2009) Meditations begin on academy status. *Times Educational Supplement,* 13.02.09

Marr, N. and Field, T. (2001) *Bullycide: death at playtime*. Didcot: Success Unlimited

Marsh, P., Rosser, E. and Harre, R. (1978) *The Rules of Disorder.* London: Routledge and Kegan Paul

Masters, B. A. (2001) Minute of silence in schools is upheld: federal judges rule law is not unconstitutional. *Washington Post,* 25.07.01

Maxwell, L. E. and Evans, G. W. (2000) The effects of noise on pre-school children's pre-reading skills. *Journal of Environmental Psychology* 20 p91-97

Mazzei, L. A. (2007) *Inhabited Silence in Qualitative Research: putting poststructural theory to work.* New York: Peter Lang

McCormack, S. (2008) Where silence is on the timetable: Quiet is key at Quaker schools. *The Independent,* 25.09.08

McGilchrist, I. (2009) *The Master and His Emissary: the divided brain and the making of the western world.* New Haven and London: Yale University Press

McMahon, D. and Mahony, D. (2011) School at prayer in Fiji. *The Meditatio Journal* Autumn(1)

Mental Health Foundation, The (2011) *Be Mindful Campaign.* URL: http://www.be mindful. co.uk/: [17.07.11]

Meighan, R., Harber, C., Barton, L., Siraj-Blatchford, I. and Walker, S. (2007) *A Sociology of Educating.* London: Continuum

Merton, T. (1974) *New Seeds of Contemplation.* New York: New Directions Publishing Corporation

Miller, R. (2008) *The Self-Organising Revolution.* Brandon: Psychology Press/Holistic Education Press

Mintz, J. and Ricci, C. (eds.) (2010) *Turning Points: 27 visionaries in education tell their own stories.* USA: Alternative Education Resource Organisation

Mochi, C. (2010) Parola di scienziati: meditare, allontana l'ansia e le malattie. *Il Venerdi di Repubblica,* 07.02.10

Montessori, M. (1990) *The Discovery of the Child.* Oxford: Clio Press Ltd

Moran, P. (2012) Deleuze and the queer ethics of an empirical education. *Studies in Philosophy and Education* online first http://rd.springer.com/article/10.1007/s11217-012-9298-3

Naish, J. (2011) How Quaker-inspired silence can revitalise your school assembly. *The Times*, 5.10.11

Naish, J. (2009) Is anyone out there listening? *The Times*, 27.10.09

Nataraja, S. (2008) *The blissful brain: neuroscience and proof of the power of meditation.* London: Gaia Thinking

National Institute for Health and Clinical Excellence (2009) *Depression: the treatment and managment of depression in adults – NICE clinical guideline 90.* NHS

NDCS (2009a) *NDCS response to Revision of Building Bulletin 93.* London: National Deaf Children's Society

NDCS (2009b) *Sounds good? A call for high-quality acoustics in schools.* London: National Deaf Children's Society

Neill, A. S. (1936) *Is Scotland Educated?* London: Routledge

Neill, A. S. (1968) *Summerhill.* Harmondsworth: Penguin

Neohumanist Education (2009) *Curriculum.* URL: http://www.nhe.gurukul.edu/curriculum. htm: [27.08.09]

Nhat Hanh, T. (1990) *Breathe! You Are Alive; sutra on the full awareness of breathing.* London: Rider

Ollin, R. (2008) Silent pedagogy and rethinking classroom practice: structuring teaching through silence rather than talk. *Cambridge Journal of Education* 38(2) p265-280

Olson, K. (2009) *Wounded by School: recapturing the joy in learning and standing up to old school culture.* New York: Teachers College Press

Orr, D. (2002) The uses of mindfulness in anti-oppressive pedagogies: philosophy and praxis. *Canadian Journal of Education* 27(4) p477-90

Osberg, D., Biesta, G. and Cilliers, P. (2008) From representation to emergence: complexity's challenge to the epistemology of schooling. *Educational Philosophy and Theory* 40(1)

Osberg, D. and Biesta, G. (2007) Beyond presence: epistemological and pedagogical implications of 'strong' emergence. *Interchange* 38(1) p31-51

Paludan, J. P. (2006) Personalised Learning 2025. In: OECD (ed.) *Personalising Education.* Paris: Centre for Educational Research and Innovation

Papert, S. (1993) *The Children's Machine: rethinking school in the age of the computer.* New York: Basic Books

Paramananda, S. (1974) *Silence as Yoga.* Calcutta: Vedanta Centre

Parkins, W. and Craig, G. (2006) *Slow Living.* Oxford: Berg

Parks, T. (2010a) *Teach Us to Sit Still.* London: Harvill Secker

Parks, T. (2010b) Try something quietly profound. *The Guardian*, 13.11.10

Paton, G. (2011) Silence is golden: how keeping quiet in the classroom can boost results. *The Telegraph*, 21.10.11

Patten, K. (1997) Teaching 'Discovering Silence'. In: Jaworski, A. (ed.) *Silence: Interdisciplinary Perspectives*. Berlin and New York: Mouton de Gruyter

Peim, N. and Flint, K. J. (2012) *Rethinking the Education Improvement Agenda: a critical philosophical approach*. London: Continuum

Pereira, A. P. (2011) *The 'discipline' of meditation with children*. URL: http://christian meditation.org.uk/public_html/downloads/WCCMNewsMay2011.pdf: [02.11.11]

Peters, R. S. and Hirst, P. H. (1970) *The Logic of Education*. London and New York: Routledge and Kegan Paul

Petrina, C. and Padovani, G. (2005) *Slow Food Revolution: da arcigola a terra madre, una nuova cultura del cibo e della vita*. Milano: Rizzoli

Picard, M. (2002) *The World of Silence*. Wichita, Kansas: Eighth Day Press

Pilkington, C. L. and Piersel, W. C. (1991) School phobia – a critical analysis of the separation anxiety theory and an alternative conceptualization. *Psychology in the Schools* 28(4) p290-303

Polanyi, M. (1974) *Personal Knowledge*. Chicago: The University of Chicago Press

Polanyi, M. (1983) *The Tacit Dimension*. Gloucester, MA: Peter Smith

Pope, D. (2001) *Doing School: how we are creating a generation of stressed out, materialistic, and miseducated students*. New Haven: Yale

Princen, T. (2010) *Treading Softly: paths to ecological order*. Cambridge, MA: The MIT Press

Prochnik, G. (2010) *In Pursuit of Silence: listening for meaning in a world of noise*. New York: Doubleday

Pruett, J. M., Nishimura, N. J. and Priest, R. (2007) The role of meditation in addiction recovery. *Counseling and Values* 52(1)

Ramirez, F. O. and Boli, J. (1987) The political construction of mass schooling: european origins and worldwide institutionalization. *Sociology of Education* 60(1) p2-17

Reda, M. M. (2009) *Between Speaking and Silence*. New York: State University of New York Press

Reps, P. (ed.) (2000) *Zen Flesh Zen Bones: a collection of Zen and pre-Zen writings* London: Penguin

Rogers, C. R. (2000) *Client-Centered Therapy*. London: Constable

Rogers, D. (2011a) Maharishi hopes DfE lets it be for school No.3. *Times Educational Supplement*, 18.11.11

Rogers, R. (2011b) The sound of silence. *The Observer*, 13.03.11

Rose, J. (2009) *Independent Review of the Primary Curriculum: final report*. Nottingham: DCSF Publications

Rowe, M. B. (1974) Pausing phenomena: influence on the quality of instruction. *Journal of Psycholinguistic Research* 3(3) p203-224

Royal Society (2011) *Brain Waves Module 2. Neuroscience: implications for education and lifelong learning.* London: The Royal Society

Sardello, R. (2008) *Silence: the mystery of wholeness.* Benson, North Carolina: Goldenstone Press

Sasso, C. and Cecla, F. I. (2010) L'invasione dei decibel. *La Repubblica*, 07.02.10

Schultz, K. (2009) *Rethinking Classroom Participation: listening to silent voices.* New York: Teachers College Press

Schwartz, J. and Maher, T. (eds.) (2006) *Trusting Children: a look at Sudbury education around the world.* Salt Lake City, Utah: Sego Lily School

Schwartz, L. (1996) *Understanding silence.* PhD Thesis, Glasgow University

Seldon, A. (2010) *The month ahead, Saturday 9th October until Sunday 7th November, the master's voice.* URL: http://www.wellingtoncollege.org.uk/newsletters/archive/mich-10/9-oct—-7-nov: [12.01.12]

Seldon, A. (2011) Stillness in Schools. *Resurgence* 269. November/December 2011, http://www.resurgence.org/magazine/article1503.html

Seligman, M. E. P. (2002) *Authentic happiness: using the new positive psychology to realize your potential for lasting fulfillment.* New York: Free Press

Semple, R. J., Lee, J., Rosa, D. and Miller, L. F. (2010) A randomized trial of Mindfulness-Based Cognitive Therapy for children: promoting Mindful attention to enhance social-emotional resiliency in children. *Journal of Child and Family Studies* 19 p218-229

Shaxson, N. (2008) *Poisoned Wells: the dirty politics of African oil.* London: Palgrave MacMillan

Sheffer, S. (1995) *A Sense of Self – listening to home schooled adolescent girls.* Portsmouth, New Hampshire: Boynton/Cook Publishers

Shepherd, J. (2011) Climate change should be excluded from curriculum, says adviser. *The Guardian*, 13.06.11

Sidorkin, A. M. (2011) On the essence of education. *Studies in Philosophy and Education* 30(5)

Siegel, D. (2006) An interpersonal neurobiology Aapproach to psychotherapy: awareness, mirror neurons, and neural plasticity in the development of well-being. *Psychiatric Annals* 36(4)

Siegel, D. (2009) *Goldie Hawn and Dan Siegel at TEDMED 2009.* URL: http://www.youtube.com/watch?v=1OdBXGHwNCk: [28.07.11]

Siegel, D. (2010) *Mindsight.* Oxford: One World Publications

Sillin, J. G. (2005) Who can speak?: silence, voice and pedagogy. In: Yelland, N. (ed.) *Critical Issues in Early Childhood Education.* Maidenhead: Open University Press

Sim, S. (2007) *Manifesto for Silence.* Edinburgh: Edinburgh University Press

Skidelsky, W. (2011) Slow down and inhabit the now: Britain enjoys a meditation boom. *The Observer,* 02.01.11

Staff Writer (2008) 'Lesbian' jibes drive 14-yr-old to suicide. *Metro*, 10.01.08

Staff Writer (2009) Warwickshire – eco event celebrates sustainability. *Times Educational Supplement*, 17.07.09

Stern, J. (2001) John Macmurray, spirituality, community and real schools. *International Journal of Children's Spirituality* 6(1) p25-39

Stronach, I. and Piper, H. (2008) Can liberal education make a comeback? The case of 'relational touch' at Summerhill School. *American Educational Research Journal* 45(1) p6-37

Sudbury Valley School (1992) *The Sudbury Valley School Experience*. Framingham, MA: Sudbury Valley School Press

Suissa, J. (2008) Lessons from a new science: on teaching happiness in schools. *Journal of Philosophy of Education* 42(3-4) p575-590

Tannen, D. and Saville-Troike, M. (eds.) (1995) *Perspectives on Silence*. Norwood, NJ: Ablex Publishing Corporation

Theresa of Avila (2004) *The Life of Saint Teresa of Avila by Herself*. London: Penguin Classics

Thomas, A. and Pattison, H. (2007) *How Children Learn at Home*. London: Continuum

Thompson, R. (2011) Letter from Campaigns Officer, British Humanist Association: 'There's science, then there's pseudoscience'. *Times Educational Supplement*, 02.12.11

Thornton, S. J. (2004) Silence on gays and lesbians in social studies curriculum. In: Flinders, D. J. and Thornton, S. J. (eds.) The Curriculum Studies Reader. Abington: RoutledgeFalmer

Thorpe, A. (2011) Three cheers for silence. *The Times Educational Supplement Scotland*, 28.10.11

Tomlinson, J. (2007) *The Culture of Speed: the coming of immediacy*. London: Sage

Tomlinson, M. (2004) *14-19 Curriculum and Qualifications Reform: final report of the working group on 14-19 reform*. Annesley: DfES Publications

Tooley, J. (2009) *The Beautiful Tree: a personal journey into how the world's poorest people are educating themselves*. Washington: Cato Institute

Topping, K. and Trickey, S. (2007) Philosophy for children: deepening learning for 10 to 12 year old pupils. *British Journal of Educational Psychology* 77 p271-288

Trafford, B. (2003) *School Councils, School Democracy, School Improvement: why, what, how?* Leicester: Secondary Heads Association

Trickey, S. and Topping, K. J. (2004) 'Philosophy for children': a systematic review. *Research Papers in Education* 19(3)

Tyack, D. and Cuban, L. (1995) *Tinkering Towards Utopia: a century of public school reform*. Cambridge, MA: Harvard University Press

UNDP (2002) *Human Development Report: deepening democracy in a fragmented world*. New York /Oxford: United Nations Development Programme von Wright, M. (2008) Why is stillness a threat against educational compliance? *Notes from seminar presentation at 'Powers of Silence' seminar.* Kristiansand: University of Oslo

von Wright, M. (2012) Silence in the asymmetry of educational relations. In: Kristiansen, A. and Hägg, H. (eds.) *Attending to Silence.* Norway: Portal

Walkerdine, V. (1985) On the regulation of speaking and silence: subjectivity, class and gender in contemporary schooling. In: Walkerdine, V., Urwin, C. and Steedman, C. (eds.) *Language, Gender and Childhood.* London: Routledge and Kegan Paul

Wall, R. B. (2005) Tai chi and mindfulness-based stress reduction in a Boston public middle school. *Journal of Pediatric Health Care* 19(4) p230-237

Walton, G. (2005) 'Bullying widespread': a critical analysis of research and public discourse on bullying. *Journal of School Violence* 4(1) p91-118

Watts, M. and Bridges, D. (2004) *Whose aspirations? What achievement? An investigation of the life and lifestyle aspirations of 16-19 year olds outside the formal educational system.* Cambridge: Association of Universities in the East of England

Weare, K. (2010) *Mindfulness; the missing piece for SEL?* URL: http://www.sharp hamtrust.org/uploads/userfiles/Mindfulness_in_SEL[1].pdf: [08.01.12]

WHO (1999) Guidelines for Community Noise. In: Berglund, B., Lindvall, T. and Schwela, D. H. (eds.). Geneva: World Health Organisation

Wilbrink, B. (1997) Assessment in historical perspective. *Studies in Educational Evaluation* 23(1) pp. 31-48

Wilce, H. (2009) Licence to chill: the primary school taking learning to another level. *The Independent*, 28.05.09

Wilkinson, R. and Pickett, K. (2009) *The Spirit Level: why more equal societies almost always do better.* London: Allen Lane

Williams, M., Teasdale, J., Segal, Z. and Kabat-Zinn, J. (2007) *The Mindful Way Through Depression: freeing yourself from chronic unhappiness.* New York: The Guilford Press

Willis, P. E. (1981) *Learning to Labour: how working class kids get working class jobs.* New York: Columbia University Press

Winzelberg, A. J. and Luskin, F. M. (1999) The effect of a meditation training in stress levels in secondary school teachers. *Stress Medicine* 15(69-77)

Wittgenstein, L. (1992) *Philosophical Investigations.* Oxford: Blackwell

Wittgenstein, L. (1993) *Tractatus Logico-Philosophicus.* Atlantic Highlands, NJ: Humanities Press International

Wolf, A. D. (2007) Renewing the silence game. *Montessori international magazine*

Woman's Hour (2011) Silence in the classroom. URL: http://www.bbc.co.uk/pro grammes/b017cb07: [24.04.12]

Wulff, F. (2011) Meditation with children: a very fruitful year. *Christian Meditation Newsletter*

Yoneyama, S. (1999) *The Japanese High School: silence and resistance.* London: Routledge

Yoneyama, S. (2000) Student discourse on tokokyohi (school phobia/refusal) in Japan: burnout or empowerment? *British Journal of Sociology of Education* 21(1) p77-94

Zembylas, M. and Michaelides, P. (2004) The sound of silence in pedagogy. *Educational Theory* 54(2)

Appendix I
Interviews

The empirical data for this book was garnered from six educationists of whom five currently work in schools. Four (UK1-4) are headteachers of thriving private schools and one is a teacher (UK5) in a similar kind of school. The sixth participant was a Head of Department in a state school (UK6) for some years and now works as a university lecturer.

UK1-4 were all interviewed in person, separately. I recorded the conversation in the case of UK2-4 and took notes for UK1 by hand at the participant's request. I interviewed UK5 by telephone and recorded the conversation, with their agreement. UK6 sent their testimony by email.

The participants were all sent an information sheet about my book beforehand, outlining the potential focus of an interview and the ethical framework I was using. Rather than working from a prior list of questions I followed my feeling about what might be particularly interesting to discuss in each case. The interviews followed a general line of enquiry about the silence in their schools and their practices but I asked additional questions to elucidate whatever seemed interesting. To a certain extent this was informed by my prior experience and observation of their schools, by comments made at an earlier exchange or during the interview. I met the headteachers and teacher via my contacts or enquiries, except for UK6 who was a colleague.

Apart from UK1, where I typed up the handwritten notes, the interviews with the headteachers were all transcribed in full (except for off topic talk) by me or a professional transcriber.

I told participants that I would anonymise their interviews, using numbers for their schools so I could raise what they were saying about silence to a level that was generalisable. I did not wish people to think that any practice was exclusive to only one type of school. The anonymity achieved by the UK1-5 labels is not a total guarantee that no interviewee or school can be recognised. This 'token' anonymity was agreed by the participants, although UK6 is wholly anonymous as their testimony is about activities long past.

The ethical procedure for the conduct of this research was checked and agreed by the Ethics Committee of the School of Education at Stirling University and was designed to follow the Code of Practice set out by the British Educational Research Association (BERA, 2004).

Appendix 2
Schools practising silence

This section features UK schools with two or more years' experience of silence in schools, who took up the invitation to list themselves. They describe their practice in their own words and voice, as I invited them to. So there is sometimes repetition about history or philosophy. However, what comes through in each instance is the individual spirit of the school or practitioner in their own style of communication.

Tonbridge School
Contact person: Richard Burnett
Address: Tonbridge, Kent, TN9 1JP
www.tonbridge-school.co.uk

Overview
Mindfulness has been taught at Tonbridge in one form or another since 2001. In 2007 Tonbridge was one of two schools (the other was Hampton School) involved in a very early study of the effectiveness of mindfulness with adolescents, done in collaboration with Professor Huppert of Cambridge University's Well-being Institute. The results were published in 2010 in the *Journal of Positive Psychology*.

Since 2009 students have been taught the 9 week .b curriculum by Richard Burnett, co-founder of the Mindfulness in Schools Project (www.mindfulnessin schools.org) and co-creator of .b, with widespread media coverage of the course in 2010. All year 10 are taught .b as part of their school timetable, with a revision class pre-GCSE in year 11 and voluntary groups after that. Tim Haynes, the school's headmaster, took part in an 8 week MBCT course, as did the Director of Sport (ex-Zimbabwe cricketer Andy Whittall), with about 25% of teachers at Ton-bridge having either taken part in an introductory mindfulness class or observed a lesson. The first parents' course took place in 2010, and the training is being ext-ended to support staff in 2011/12.

St James Senior Girls' School

Contact person: Laura Hyde
Address: Earsby Street, London W14 8SH
www.stjamesgirls.co.uk

Overview

Meditation has been a central part of school life since the foundation of St James Senior Girls' School in 1975. We continue to learn and adapt our approach to the offer of periods of silence according to experience and the response of our pupils. All pupils (10-18 years) engage in two periods of silence every day in which they may meditate, contemplate, silently pray or simply 'be', according to their own spiritual inclination or tradition. Pupils may be introduced to a classical form of mantra meditation from India, if they so wish and some come with their own method of meditation. In addition, we have a short pause before and after each lesson in which pupils can let go of past impressions or concerns about the future; this leaves them free to attend. Regular recourse to simple quiet has a stabilising and strengthening effect on the mind and emotions, allowing the discovery of inner freedom from the impact of passing experience. Girls enjoy some ease of being. Relationships are enhanced through greater gentleness and sensitivity to each others' conditions.

St James Junior School

Contact person: Catherine Thomlinson
Address: Earsby Street, London W148SH
www.stjamesjuniorschool.co.uk

Overview

Meditation has been a central part of the school life since the foundation of St James Schools in 1975. In the Junior School, meditation is offered from Yr 6 and stillness is practised by all the children age 4 to 11. A moment of stillness and quiet is taken at the beginning and end of every activity, providing a space for reflection, connection or simply being. Stillness increases children's ability to attend and being able to attend and concentrate is possibly one of the greatest gifts anyone can receive. Most of the teachers at St James Junior School meditate.

St James Senior Boys' School

Contact person: David Boddy
Address: Ashford, Surrey, TW153DZ
www.stjamesschools.co.uk

Overview

Meditation and quiet time practices have been central to the educational philosophy of St James schools since they were founded in 1975. There are two main practices: a dedicated Quiet Time period for ten minutes twice a day, and a short 'Pause' (for about 30 seconds) before and at the end of every activity.

Pupils may learn a form of mantra-based meditation if they wish (in the Senior Boys, about 30% do), instructed by the School of Meditation in Central London. Other pupils are invited to use the period to pray or contemplate statements from scriptural texts, or practice a series of mindfulness breathing exercises. The golden rule is that no boy should disturb the peace of another. On three mornings a week, the Quiet Time is held collectively as part of the school assembly; on the other two days, it is held in class groups. Every afternoon, straight after registration, the second Quiet Time period is held, also in class groups. The Quiet Time periods are supported by philosophy discussions in each class, centred on the idea that each person has within them a divine, conscious and intelligent spirit, which is full of love and creativity. We call this the Philosophy of Oneness. Teachers meet daily and spend a brief silent period together, plus listen to an eclectic selection of short spiritual readings before dealing with the day's business. All the great religions are represented in both the pupil and staff bodies.

Similar practices take place in our sister school (St James Senior Girls, Olympia, London). Our junior school (also in Olympia) introduces the children to the 'Pause'. Those who wish to learn to meditate with a mantra can do so from age 10.

Pupils in the senior schools are now mentoring younger pupils in the various practices and deriving excellent benefits from that. We hope this continues to develop.

Quaker Schools in the UK and Ireland

Ackworth School
Pontefract, West Yorkshire WF7 7LT
Tel 01977 611401
www.ackworthschool.com
admissions@ackworthschool.com

Bootham School
York YO30 7BU
Tel 01904 623261
www.boothamschool.com
enquiries@boothamschool.com

Friends' School
6 Magheralave Road, Lisburn BT28
3BH
Tel 028 9266 2156
www.friendsschoollisburn.org.uk
info@friends.lisburn.ni.sch.uk

Friends' School
Saffron Walden, Essex CB11 3EB
Tel 01799 525351
www.friends.org.uk
info@friends.org.uk

Leighton Park
Reading RG2 7ED
Tel 0118 987 9608
www.leightonpark.com
info@leightonpark.com

The Mount School
Dalton Terrace, York YO24 4DD
Tel 01904 667 500
www.mountschoolyork.co.uk
enquiries@mount.n-yorks.sch.uk

Newtown School
Newtown Road, Waterford, Ireland
Tel +353 51 860 200
www.newtownschool.ie
info@newtownschool.ie

Sibford School
Sibford Ferris, Banbury, Oxfordshire
OX15 5QL
Tel 01295 781203
www.sibford.oxon.sch.uk
admissions@sibfordschool.co.uk

Sidcot School
Winscombe, North Somerset BS25
1PD
Tel 01934 845212
www.sidcot.org.uk
admissions@sidcot.org.uk

Overview relevant to the Quaker schools listed above (joint statement)
Each of the Quaker Schools holds regular silent Meetings for Worship, in keeping with the practice of the Religious Society of Friends. This collective period of silence provides a powerful vehicle for the whole school community to come together, while allowing individuals to gather and explore their own thoughts. A text might be offered at a point in the Meeting to provide a focus for individual thought, or individuals may feel moved to speak. We do not think that our students necessarily use this time for deeply spiritual thought, but the great strength of Quaker schools is that they encourage pupils to be comfortable with themselves, to think independently and express themselves clearly. The silence contributes to the pupils' ability to engage in higher level thinking and adopt a state of mindfulness as they navigate their way through their time at school.

Shorter periods of silence are integral to the daily life of the schools, such as before meals, meetings or to open and close events. It is amazing how quickly pupils get used to falling into silence without being told, and how soon they learn the value of the silences that punctuate the day. The overall atmosphere of quiet reflection is not disturbed by the ringing of bells between lessons but there is still a sense of energy and purpose in the schools.

***

There are other schools in the UK and elsewhere which have been practising with silence for many years. Some of these schools are mentioned in this book, particularly in chapter five. If a school with established silence practice would like to appear in any subsequent editions of this book, they are welcome to contact the author directly.

Appendix 3

**There is a website to accompany this book:
www.silenceinschools.org**

More weblinks relating to silence practices[1]

Silence practices in schools

www.davidlynchfoundation.org/schools/

www.thehawnfoundation.org

www.mindspace.org.uk/category/education/

www.garrisoninstitute.org (see: initiative- contemplation and education)

www.latchmerej.kingston.sch.uk/meditation.htm

www.tmeducation.org/

www.consciousnessbasededucation.org.uk/index.shtml

www.krishnamurti-and-education.org/schools.htm

www.mindspace.org.uk/meditate/education/

www.psychologist.ms/mis.htm

www.mindfuleducation.org/

www.mindfulschools.org/

Silence practices with children

www.t-m.org.uk/meditation-children-and-teenagers.shtml

www.mindfulkids.wordpress.com/

www.handsonscotland.co.uk/ (go to flourishing/mindfulness)

www.stillquietplace.com/

1 Apart from the site I manage www.silenceinschools.org, I list these sites without having affiliation to, or involvement with any of them. Nor anyone involved in them (this is certainly the case at the time this book was published) and I am not responsible for what they may contain. They look interesting. There are many others of interest not listed here. Some of these sites have good links to other sites of potential interest. All the sites were accessed in January 2012.

Mindfulness for health and well-being campaign

www.bemindful.co.uk

Mindfulness research

University of Bangor

www.bangor.ac.uk/mindfulness/

University of Oxford

www.oxfordmindfulness.org/

www.mbct.co.uk

University of Massachusetts Medical School

www.umassmed.edu/cfm/home/

University College Los Angeles

www.marc.ucla.edu

Mind & Life Institute

www.mindandlife.org

General sites

www.mindfulnet.org

www.contemplativemind.org

www.mindfulness-works.com

www.puresilence.org

Index